SCHOOL MARKETING MANUAL
for the
Digital Age
3rd edition

Attempts have been made to contact copyright holders or to abide by all the Terms and Conditions associated with copyright available on each website. If there are any errors or omissions, copyright holders are asked to contact Great Developments Pty Ltd so that acknowledgements or adjustments can be updated. Other companies wishing to be included in the next edition should contact the publisher.

Published in 2011
by Great Developments Pty Ltd
20 Aldrin Avenue
Benowa, Gold Coast, Queensland, Australia 4217
ABN: 13133435168
USA-EIN: 98-0689457
http://marketschools.com

1st Edition published	2008 as School Marketing Handbook: Easy to Use Guide to Market Your School
2nd Edition published	2009 as School Marketing e-Handbook: Easy to Use Guide to Market Your School
3rd Edition published	2010 as School Marketing Manual for the Digital Age (3rd ed) – ebook edition
	2011 as School Marketing Manual for the Digital Age (3rd ed) – paperback edition

Paperback edition printed by CreateSpace, part of the Amazon group of companies, USA.

Copyright © Great Developments Pty Ltd, 2011
ISBN-10: 098061077x
EAN-13: 9780980610772

National Library of Australia Cataloguing-in-Publication entry

Author: Foster, Bryan, 1957-
Title: School marketing manual for the digital age / Bryan Foster.
Edition: 3rd ed.
ISBN: 9780980610772 (pbk)
Notes: Includes bibliographical references and index
Subjects: Schools--Marketing--Handbooks, manuals, etc.
Schools--Public relations—Australia--Handbooks, manuals, etc.
Dewey Number: 659.29371

SCHOOL MARKETING MANUAL

for the

Digital Age

3rd edition

BRYAN FOSTER

Table of Contents

    SMP Overview Sample
    Analysis of the SMP
    Be Ethical
    Who Needs a SMP?

    Overview
    Full / Part-Time or Shared Role
    SMM Skills Needed
    School Response to SMM

    Overview
    Support Cluster — School Leadership Team
    Support Cluster of SMMs
    System-Level Support and Regional Cluster

Front Desk Monitor — Best Use of...

About the Author

Bryan Foster has been marketing Catholic schools for 20 years, since 1994 in a city secondary school and for 4 years in the 1980s as a principal in two country primary schools.

He is presently the Director of his company, Great Developments Pty Ltd — an internet publishing company, which specializes in books and e-books for marketing schools and churches. Bryan maintains his association with schools through his secondary teaching position at Aquinas College.

A highly ethical approach to marketing, and passion for marketing the Catholic school, was formed as a result of his extensive Religious Education teaching experience in Catholic primary and secondary schools in the city and country.

He was the Marketing Manager at Aquinas College, a secondary co-educational college on the Gold Coast, in what is arguably the most difficult school marketing region in Australia. He was also the school's Assistant Principal Religious Education (APRE).

Bryan was seconded to Brisbane Catholic Education for the 2008 school year as the Catching Fire: Evangelization and Spiritual Formation Education Officer.

He has held various senior and middle school management positions: a primary school Principal in two schools, APRE in secondary school and Years 9, 11 and 12 Coordinator.

He holds a:
- Master of Education from the Australian Catholic University in Sydney
- Bachelor of Education}
- Graduate Diploma in Religious Education}
- Diploma of Teaching} from McAuley Teachers College in Brisbane
- Diploma of Religious Education from the Institute of Faith Education, Brisbane.

He has taught for over 30 years in Catholic schools from Years 1 to 12.

Bryan has assisted many school marketing coordinators. He is considered highly by Brisbane Catholic Education and throughout the years has assisted their marketing personnel.

His wife, eldest daughter and son all teach in Catholic primary schools, while his younger daughter attends a Catholic secondary school.

Bryan Foster has also written the next edition of his popular church marketing e-handbook. The _Church Marketing Manual for the Digital Age (2nd ed)_ (2010) adds a whole new dimension from his experiences with digital marketing. This is combined with a complete update of the regular contemporary and traditional school marketing strategies.

His leadership roles within the Church also include:

- South Coast Deanery Pastoral Council, Chair
- St Mary's Parish Pastoral Council, Coomera, Chair
- Surfers Paradise Parish Pastoral Council, Surfers Paradise, Secretary
- St Kevin's School, Parents and Friends Association, Benowa, President

All of these are on the Gold Coast, Australia.

Bryan lives on the Gold Coast with his family and is an active member of his local Parish.

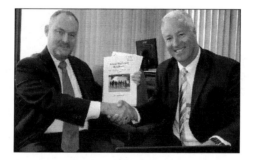

"I have known Bryan Foster for over twenty years. Bryan is a committed and highly professional educator and administrator. In particular he has demonstrated great leadership in the area of school marketing and promotions. He has always been willing to share his experience and expertise with colleagues."

— David Hutton, Executive Director of Catholic Education - _Archdiocese of Brisbane_

Acknowledgements

A successful School Marketing Plan is only possible with the support of the key stakeholders within the school. I would like to offer my sincere thanks to a most remarkable group of people: the staff, parents, students and priests of Aquinas College, Southport, St Joseph's, Tara, and St Mary's, Goondiwindi. Their support, encouragement and ideas have been instrumental in developing each school's successful School Marketing Plan (SMP) over all the years: 1982 — 86 and 1994 onwards.

The three Principals at Aquinas College since 1994, Terry Enright, Sr Nancy Freddi rsm and Maryanne Finder, particularly need special mention and thanks. Terry Enright's invitation in 1994 was to take on this new and unknown role in a rather interesting climate of change. Sr Nancy Freddi, Principal from 1999 to 2004, considerably expanded the role and support of the School Marketing Coordinator (SMC). Maryanne Finder, present Principal from 2005, maintained the high order and respect of the person and the role and encouraged the School Marketing Manager (SMM) unconditionally. Many thanks for the experiences and support, these are very much appreciated.

I have also very much enjoyed my association with key marketing people within Brisbane Catholic Education, in particular, in the early days, Michael Sullivan, Manager Communications and Marketing and more recently Bernadette Kreutzer whose various roles included Acting Manager Communications and Marketing, along with their highly credentialed staff. John Phelan, present Manager Communications and Marketing, BCE, has been a wonderful supporter.

I am particularly appreciative of the tremendous support given to me by David Hutton, Executive Director, Brisbane Catholic Education, in this and other roles over the past twenty years.

Finally a warm-hearted and special thanks to my wife, Karen, and three children, Leigh-Maree, Andrew and Jacqueline, along with my parents, Frank and Mary, and other family members who have supported and encouraged me in this role over so many years. Your love has always been so necessary for the success.

Preface

The development of two key resources — the 'SMA: School Marketing' interactive website and the *School Marketing Manual for the Digital Age (3rd ed)* (2011) paperback, came about to share outcomes and skills gained **from the many years' experience marketing schools at the 'school-face'.** Being on staff within these schools, I was able to see firsthand what was required and then to do something about these needs.

We need to use all appropriately available resources to get our message to as many people as we possibly can in effective, attractive and enjoyable ways. This new *School Marketing Manual for the Digital Age* (2011) is the 3rd edition of the popular *School Marketing e-Handbook: Easy to Use Guide to Market Your School* (published 2009).

Feedback resulting from the original SMA website, which has been continually developed over the years since its inception, would suggest that this website, which houses this original e-book, plays an important part in marketing the school for a growing group of like-minded people.

The SMA website at http://marketschools.com/ has included an array of interactive components, which would assist with the marketing of your school. Two popular interactive aspects are the *Blogs* (currently 100+ posts) and the *Hints and Tips*. These are regularly updated. Readers are encouraged to offer their own thoughts publicly through the Blogs or privately to the author through the Contact Us.

If you would like to receive RSS feeds of any of the webpage updates e.g. *Blogs, Hints and Tips, Specials* and *News*, just click on the RSS orange symbol, which is either on the webpage or above on the toolbar, and follow the instructions. RSS feeds update you once something new is added to each selected webpage. (More on RSS in e-book)

Introduction

The *School Marketing Manual for the Digital Age (3rd ed)* (2011) contains a major digital section for marketing schools in the modern age — over 100 pages. 90+ screenshots of actual internet pages are included to assist. The other contemporary marketing methods have also been updated. A combination of the digital and other contemporary and traditional methods is critical for a successful school marketing plan. This book begins with a sample school marketing plan overview and concludes with an invitation to begin creating your School Marketing Action Plan on the pages provided.

When the school marketing e-book is downloaded from the website and opened on your computer, with your internet connection on, you will be able to link directly from the e-book to various websites — over 130 website links are included. As an example, if you hold down the Control key and do a left click while hovering over the blue link e-Book you will go directly to the webpage describing in detail the new *School Marketing Manual for the Digital Age (3rd ed)* e-book. If you only have this paperback version of this e-book, just copy the links into your internet browser.

The screenshot images taken directly of various websites, form part of this instruction manual, to assist you with seeing what various sites offer. These also show what you would see if you progressed with using these sites, or becoming a member of those sites with certain membership privileges. These memberships are mostly free of charge.

This book has an **easy to use approach**. It is written in a **clear, concise, summarized, point-format**, which **engages and motivates the reader.**

Step-by-step strategies and instructions enable the School Marketing Manager to work toward the implementation of the School Marketing Plan in the best way the SMM feels possible within his / her context.

Apart from the digital age challenges, which have been simply explained, another common challenge is **dealing with the traditional mass media**. This challenge is addressed through explaining how best to use the media to the school's advantage, as well as how best to market the school through the media. Another is the challenge to effectively work through the **production of various marketing resources**. These are covered throughout.

School Marketing Plan

Preparing an effective, efficient and creative School Marketing Plan is essential for success:

1. This book begins with a Sample OVERVIEW of a School Marketing Plan.

2. Each aspect of this Plan is dealt with in considerable detail throughout the Manual.

3. Your Action Plan is then called for at the end of the text.

School Marketing (SMA) Website

As well as the book, the interactive 'SMA: School Marketing' website aims to continually engage the reader as the website grows and develops according to the needs of those interested in this school marketing website.

Free membership of the site offers the opportunity to be fully informed as new developments occur. To join the SMA website just hold down the control key and click on *Join Now* or add http//:marketschools.com to your web browser.

The website contains the e-book *School Marketing Manual for the Digital Age (3rd ed)* in the *Online Shop* plus regularly updated: *Blogs, Hints and Tips* and *News* items.

Interactive contact may be made through the *Blogs* or *Contact Us*.

The book overview is detailed at *e-Books*, detail on the author is at *Bryan Foster*, and there are pages on *Specials*, *Testimonials,* and *Sponsorship*.

There are also a *Gallery* of Photos and a gallery of *Videos,* as well as the *Site Search* option on each page.

Many screenshots have been taken from this 'SMA: School Marketing' website and my private social networking sites, etc, and used in the 'School Marketing - Internet Applications…' chapter. These are used to help clarify various aspects to do with websites, the internet and all that both offer and are not used to what may appear as self-promotion. This concentration on just key websites occurred due to the difficulty of gaining copyright permission from a larger number of websites.

School Marketing Plan Overview

School Marketing Plan Overview Sample

Define what you have to offer:
- vision and mission, personnel, curriculum, sacramental / prayer life, pastoral and welfare support programs, religious / arts / sport education, facilities, extra-curricular activities, etc
- specific ages and groups catered for — from infants to senior secondary
- future plans — programs, staffing, facilities, etc.

Define your target group:
- through surveys, observations, experience, gifts and talents available / needed
- proximity to / involvement with school educational institutes — elementary / primary, secondary and tertiary + any churches
- any expansion — programs, facilities, staffing

Budget:
- realistically support the school marketing plan
- be flexible and open to growth and change as the needs arise
- continually develop over time through needs and experiences

Personnel and Talents available — including School Marketing Manager

Develop School Marketing Aims and Objectives — from previous information

Select Marketing Strategies:
- School Marketing Relationships
- School Marketing Resources (including branding, advertising)
- Using the Media
    * Internet and other Contemporary methods
    * Both for Free (Media Releases / Editorial, etc) and for
    * Fee (Advertising)

Evaluation

School Marketing Plan
School Marketing Manager

School Marketing Plan
School Marketing Manager

The PLAN. The Manager. The spend. The support. The evaluation.

The right person managing the right marketing plan, being given a realistic budget and support and using continual evaluation techniques and feedback are high priorities for a successful marking plan within your school.

This chapter gets to the heart of these critical decisions. Often tough decisions need to be made and hopefully this section helps ease that concern.

Big or small budgets can both have varying degrees of success.

Know your market and its needs and develop plans accordingly.

A longer term plan often eases that initial budget constraint. Success often leads to more success. Decision makers become open to more appropriate budgets.

Headings

School Marketing Plan Overview Sample

School Marketing Manager
School Marketing Manager Support Clusters
Branding
Professionalism
Budget
School Surveys
School Marketing Plan Evaluation
Regional Marketing Plan (RMP)

School Marketing Plan

A successful School Marketing Plan (SMP) is critical to a successful school!
Be well prepared!
Plan!

School Marketing Plan Overview Sample

Define what you have to offer:
- vision and mission, personnel, curriculum, sacramental / prayer life, pastoral and welfare support programs, religious / arts / sport education, facilities, extra-curricular activities, etc
- specific ages and groups catered for - from infants to senior secondary
- future plans — programs, staffing, facilities, etc

Define your target group:
- through surveys, observations, experience, gifts and talents available / needed
- proximity to / involvement with school educational institutes — elementary / primary, secondary and tertiary + any churches
- any expansion — programs, facilities, staffing

Budget:
- realistically support the school marketing plan
- be flexible and open to growth and change as the needs arise
- continually develop over time through needs and experiences

Personnel and Talents available - including School Marketing Manager

Develop School Marketing Aims and Objectives - from previous information

Select Marketing Strategies:
- School Marketing Relationships
- School Marketing Resources (including branding, advertising)
- Using the Media
    * Internet and other Contemporary methods
    * Both for Free (Media Releases / Editorial, etc) and for Fee (Advertising)

Evaluation

Analysis of the School Marketing Plan

- The School Principal is ultimately responsible for the SMP.
- The School Marketing Plan is based on the School's Vision and Mission Statement.
- A SMP is the plan used to market the school to the community. The community includes all people who know, or those who you want to know, about the school. These include the general public in your catchment region, parents, potential families, school staff, parish staff, other schools' staff especially from feeder schools, present and past students, parents, etc.
- The SMP includes the strategies used within a defined budget.
- The plan is used to inform all stakeholders, and other targeted groups, of the benefits and successes of the school.
- It also informs about aspects which may be of interest.
- It also needs to plan for issues which may arise of a controversial nature.
- The plan should inform and emphasize the real nature of the school and the direction the school is planning or presently implementing.
- A realistic budget is part of the SMP.
- Marketing is relatively inexpensive when viewed in the terms of the potential gains made — reputation, new parents, supportive present parents, enrolments, etc.
- The SMP can benefit from the combination of views of staff and others associated with the school community.
- In the initial stages of developing the school's first real plan it is often best to include a variety of interest groups for gaining ideas and suggestions about how best to market your school. These thoughts may then be used as felt necessary.
- The School Principal needs input and has the overall responsibility to implement the plan.

SMP Evaluation

The SMP should be evaluated at least yearly and appropriate adjustments made for the following year. Changes may need to be made throughout the year depending on changing circumstances.

A SMP is not...

A successful School Marketing Plan is a lot more than the school's stationery and newsletter.

It should avoid 'dressing-up' the school in a way which cannot be supported.

Be ethical ...

Apart from being unethical, more than likely, any unethical aspects would eventually become apparent as being incorrect to the stakeholders and others.

This would have an adverse impact on the school's reputation and hence parents' and community's involvement.

Who needs a School Marketing Plan?

All schools need a School Marketing Plan.

Informing the community is seen by most schools to be an important aspect of their ministry and mission.

It also leads to the best promoters of the school.

A SMP may be as simple or as complex as needed to achieve the desired outcomes.

The plan is needed whether:

- a school presently has a large enrolment base or
- it is about to re/open or
- it is losing students.

The best time to market a school is when it is successful.

At this stage there are so many approaches which
may be taken to highlight the benefits.

However, it usually becomes an issue when enrolment numbers
are dropping or when a new school is opening need by.

At this stage a specifically targeted program is required.

Don't be caught out!

School Marketing Manager

Overview

> The School Principal will often delegate this School Marketing Manager (SMM) role to a school staff member.
>
> Full-time, Part-time or shared? The Principal's decision...
>
> However, it is best not to lose sight of employing the best person for this position.

> The School Marketing Manager will be responsible for the School Marketing Plan and responsible to the School Principal.

Full / Part-Time or Shared Role

Most SMMs would be part time in this position these days. Budgetary restraints would basically necessitate this. These people would combine this role with their other primary role, usually that of Assistant / Deputy Principal or School Manager.

To share the role, I believe, could be detrimental to it. Having someone knowing everything there is to know about was has occurred, is being planned for and involved with the future implementation of the School Marketing Plan is a definite advantage.

> I feel that the time is coming when an individual school or at least a combination of schools within a certain region / religious order / system will employ a full-time SMM.

SMM Skills Needed

The person who takes on this role will need to:

- be interested in the area of marketing and preferably passionate about it
- be a person of integrity
- be able to base the SMP on the School's Vision and Mission statement
- be aware of the marketing needs of a particular School
- have good interpersonal skills
- be able to build professional relationships with key stakeholders, members of the media and various local business personnel
- have a creative flare and appreciation of what 'catches the eye' of the targeted audiences
- have good literary skills
- have good computer skills, particularly with creative AV software packages and internet usage, or at least an appreciation of these along with other staff members or parents who would implement the software packages under your direction
- have a good appreciation of the internet and be able to implement all that this means of communication offers your particular school
- be capable of developing and implementing a viable budget
- be keen to learn and develop more successful forms of marketing and marketing skills.

School Response to SMM

The school personnel will need to:

- be open to various forms of marketing
- be willing to try other strategies, particularly successful strategies from different schools
- provide an appropriate budget to allow for the broadness and depth needed for the implementation of a successful SMP
- give appropriate time for the SMM to develop and implement the SMP
- support the SMM in this difficult area
- give time to the SMM for professional development to gain appropriate or advanced skills to implement the SMP
- allow the SMM to access the use of specialist IT personnel who may be needed to assist with various aspects of the role.

Support Clusters

All SMMs need support no matter their perceived proficiency or experience.

Overview

One of the best forms of support cluster may include each school's SMM, School Principal, Leadership Team members, selected Staff, Parents and Friends / Citizens Association and School Board.

Another support is a cluster of SMMs, usually within local proximity.

Either support cluster could benefit from inviting input from other specialists be they from other schools, system authorities, school employing authorities or other consultants.

Input on current marketing practices from within that cluster and / or by offering suggestions for improvement would be beneficial.

Support Cluster - School Leadership Team

The School Principal should always be an integral part of any SMP.

The School Principal, along with the school's Leadership Team, would normally be a wonderful support structure for the SMM.

To have gifted people literally within earshot of one another and able to have ideas bounced off each other, and opinions and ideas shared, would be beneficial.

The School Principal and Leadership Team should have confidence in the SMM and allow this person to develop the SMP without interference. This, however, needs to be done in consultation with the School Principal and maybe also with the other school Leadership Team members.

The SMM would initially need to gain the trust of the School Principal and Leadership Team.

Time, professional development and the experience of successfully completing and implementing a SMP may be integral to gaining this support.

Support Clusters of SMMs

> Often SMMs feel that all schools, even those of the same denomination, are rivals.
>
> This is most likely far from the truth.

> The more similar schools work together, in this case from the marketing perspective, the more proficient and successful each one should be.

It is believed that the old adage is correct:

> 'The star team is better than a team of stars'.

Regular meetings of SMMs, where successful and non-successful strategies of marketing are discussed and possible solutions espoused, would be of benefit to each school involved.

These meetings could also include shared creative thinking time on possible strategies along with resource development for each particular school.

System-Level Support and Clusters

School systemic support would be available to many schools. This may be done on a one to one basis i.e. the school and systemic personnel, or as a cluster of schools along with systemic personnel.

> Using the combined expertise of the system, along with any budgetary assistance, could be of substantial value to each school.

The system would most likely employ experienced marketing people and journalists.

The system may be able to supply a budget to assist schools, particularly those in need.

The initial onus may be on schools to approach the system's Communication and Marketing Manager. Be clear with your proposed needs or queries.

A first time SMM may make this approach early on to gain initial momentum and advice. They may also gain financial support to kick start the marketing process.

> Once the process has begun, these SMMs could use the other support structures mentioned above plus resources like this e-book for guidance and assistance.

Branding

Branding is often a person's first contact with the school. It is usually a visual image seen. It may also be a verbal input.

Branding's importance must not be underestimated.

First impressions do count!

First Impressions

The first impression may be gained from the following:

- Website design
- Welcome by office staff / Office decor etc
- Prospectus / Information Pack - cover, pages and inclusions
- Uniform of students and office staff
- Stationery received
- e/i-Newsletter, newsletter or newsletter design and front page content
- Telephone call response by office staff / voicemail response / telephone transfer instructions / dedicated line for upcoming events recording, etc
- White and Yellow pages listings
- Advertisement in newspaper or magazine, radio, etc
- e/i Flyer or Flyer
- Student or staff at school
- Reputations of school as espoused from someone within the community

The branding of the school needs to be well considered and representative of the school's vision and mission.
It needs to show how the school is to be seen within the community.

Uniformity

Branding needs uniformity to be a powerful, positive tool.

Mixing and matching branding causes a weak and disjointed image to be apparent.

This is to the disadvantage of the school in a number of ways. The confusing images distract and hence do not leave the desired impact.

The school may be seen itself as disjointed and 'not together' and hence causing various follow-up difficulties.

Key Branding Areas

- **Key <u>primary areas</u> of branding** include:

  - Colors
  - Logo / emblem
  - Motto / Catch phrase
  - Uniform design
  - Graphics and page layout
  - Key words to epitomize the school

Colors may vary according to the purpose i.e. outside colors of the school may differ to the inside colors and these may differ from stationery and advertising colors.

To have the same colors everywhere can become overbearing.
However, there would be less of a difficulty with soft plain colors,
but these colors often aren't strong enough for stationery and advertising.

It is important though that those colors selected for each area, inside and
outside, along with stationery and advertising are simple, matching and
constant throughout that particular usage.

- These following areas then form the basis for the **<u>secondary areas</u> of branding**, including:

- Stationery design, which would include page graphics and layouts of school details
- Logo and motto inclusion on uniforms
- Website design
- e/i-Newsletter and Newsletter design
- Covers and page layouts for school produced information booklets and brochures (e/i-booklets, e/i-flyers and e/i-brochures)
- Advertisement designs, including for the media, as well as posters, flyers, booklets
- Layout of front office
- Welcoming introduction for telephone answering / voicemails
- Welcoming at office front counter
- School DVD / CD graphics
- Key verbal phrases for radio, DVD / CD and telephone on-hold

- The following form the basis for **tertiary use of branding**, including:
  - How the various secondary forms will be used
  - Various combinations of secondary forms

Branding Changes

Evaluation of primary, secondary and tertiary branding forms is essential.

Branding needs to be thoroughly considered as it is imperative to maintain the overall branding and most specific forms for a period of years.

Major changes with branding should not occur at least for three to five years (unless the initial branding failed).

The successful images created and regularly reinforced within the minds of people from the branding are highly valuable. Think of major brands that seem to be almost eternal e.g. McDonald's and Coca Cola.

Schools are by no means within this category for financial outlay, outside consultants or market-share, however with good branding each school is a small microcosm and capable of being every bit as successful within its own demographic as the large corporations.

Changes may be needed within any specific branding period if some aspects of branding have found to be unsuccessful.

Changes will usually cause large amounts of wasted time, resources and funding.

It is best to be wise before any change is needed.

Creativity of Design

Seeking advice from other successful schools, systemic marketing personnel, or in some cases consultants for these schools, is a very good start.

Try to be original as much a possible, within your own market!

It is best not to 'copy', or be too similar to, other schools' branding.

By all means take those aspects which would suit your particular school and adapt these to your particular needs.

However, schools may benefit from similarities with schools both in and not in their own region.

A uniformity of theme within a region or religious order can work well when done properly and with the correct appreciation of the 'market'.

… with good branding, each school is a small microcosm and capable of being every bit as successful within its own demographic as the large corporations…

Professionalism

Staff - Leadership Team, Teaching and Other Administrative/Grounds Staff + Volunteers

> The **professional image** presented by the whole school community employed within the school, as well as volunteers, is essential to a successful SMP.

This includes everything from **professional dress and behavior** through to **teaching styles, respect for students and staff** and **subject / administrative knowledge**.

Name Tags, which are school branded and clearly readable, should be worn by all staff. This adds to the sense of unity and to the security of the students and staff within the school.

Business Cards produced according to the school's branding style and incorporating essential details for key personnel need to be available for staff interacting with the public. These need to be non-busy and easily readable.

Students

Student Uniforms are a key aspect of tone setting for the student body and school community. An attractive and highly functional uniform suitable for various climates and community expectations will improve the public's appreciation of the school enormously. Never underestimate the power of the school uniform.

Uniforms must also be worn properly. The **Uniform and Behavior Code** should include all aspects and not just the fabric. Include such detail as to how the fabric should be worn, how and when a hat should be worn, shoe types and cleanliness, hairstyles and neatness, jewelry expectations; as well as the general behavioral expectations of students, etc.

Hygiene issues are also a part of this professionalism. Being clean and tidy, having hair cared for, using deodorant, etc, all have an impact on the public's perception of the school.

We should be careful not to let these uniform code aspects of school life dominate such that the key areas of learning and enjoying quality school time are overshadowed.

Budget

A successful School Marketing Plan needs a well funded School Marketing Budget.

Mmm ... Money time!

This is probably the most controversial aspect of any SMP.

Overview

Various people within each school community have differing views on the amount which should be afforded to the School Marketing Budget (SMB).

School Principals and School Managers need to be aware that the implementation of a good SMP would inevitably drive up community engagement and enrolment numbers!

In today's dollar values spending $20 - $40000 on an average SMB for an average sized independent school (of between 600 and 900 students) would be a good investment.

This would need to be proportionately reviewed according to overall School Budget, the number of enrolments and the overall need of the school to build and maintain enrolment numbers.

When the SMP is being developed for a specified year, key stakeholders, particularly the School Principal, School Manager and the SMM, need to assess the budget requirements.

The budget will have a significant impact on a SMP for any year.

The SMB includes all areas of the SMP which incur expenses.

Invest During Good Times

Good times are the best times to invest.
This enables the school's reputation to be enhanced considerably.

Resting on the laurels of the past can become an expensive exercise when the reputation is forgotten or when a new challenge comes from other competing interests, including other schools and distractions within society.

However, all schools need to market themselves at whatever stage of
the success cycle at which they find themselves.
Don't give up in the tough times –
all schools will experience these throughout their history.

Shared SMPs – Regionalized or Localized

Shared SMPs across a number of schools may be another way of efficiently budgeting.

This could be **regionalized** e.g.:

- a combined regional budget to be shared amongst schools or
- a RMM (Regional Marketing Manager) implementing the whole marketing plan for the region and individual schools, which are only required to develop their own essentials such as newsletters.

Or it may be a number of **localized schools** working together and sharing the budget.

A shared budget may see different schools marketing specific aspects for the cluster e.g.

- one may concentrate on Arts / Sport Education within the cluster
- another may market the varying sorts of key curriculum and extra-curricular areas on offer and differing times for each
- another may emphasize the pastoral, welfare and social justice aspects within the cluster.

For some schools this may be the only way to begin marketing or to maintain a SMP in any form what-so-ever.

Caution

Even though this may appear to save financially, it takes away from the individual uniqueness of each school.

Marketing is often more successful when emphasizing a uniqueness.

Surveys

Surveys are often a good way to discover the views and needs of various stakeholders and of prospective parents and students.

Aims and Sample Questions

If the surveyed group believes that they will be listened to, and that the survey isn't an onerous one, then a greater percentage of quality responses will occur.

Simple questions will often elicit the best results.

Sample questions might be:

- What do you like best about (name) school?
- What improvements could be made?
- Other suggestions?

Other more explicit questions could be asked, and depending on the audience, may be of benefit, however, in most cases it is best to KIS (Keep It Simple).

Feeder Schools

Surveying the various feeder schools of a particular school should point the school in the right direction. The views of staff, parents and students of the schools are an invaluable aid as to how the school is perceived and of areas needing improvement.

Students, Staff and Parents

Students in Years 4/5-6/7 would be another good target group for this type of survey.

Staff and parents from your school could be surveyed on the perceived strengths and weaknesses of the school. Negative responses should be explained. Once again KIS would apply.

Discussion Groups

Following the survey, or in addition to the survey, Discussion Groups are often beneficial. Key stakeholders form the group/s.

Select an experienced facilitator / chairperson.

Be open to frank discussion. Be accommodating and respectful.

You will most likely need to make it clear that you are open to considering all views but the final decisions rest with the School Principal.

Varied responses will be inevitable.

It is the School Principal's and CMM's role to rank order responses and take on board those which are relevant and practical.

Survey vs. SMP Evaluation

These surveys are in addition to the SMP Evaluation.

The survey is concentrating on the perceived strengths and weaknesses of the school itself.

The SMP Evaluation is evaluating the school's marketing plan for that year.

The surveys are held as needed.

The SMP Evaluation is best conducted at the same time of the any year. This may be mid-year and away from the major school or sacramental events.

Online Surveys - Weblinks

An approach developing quite quickly these days is the online survey, which often has a free option.

There are a number of internet companies offering various surveys. An internet search of 'online survey tools' will gain a number of options to explore.

Two examples are 'polldaddy' and 'SurveyMonkey' available at:
http://www.polldaddy.com/ and http://www.surveymonkey.com/

Remember to read their Terms and Conditions fully before proceeding with usage!

An email from SurveyMonkey outlines their approach for both free and fee accounts. I include it for your information – dated 10 February, 2010:

Welcome to SurveyMonkey.com, and thanks for signing up for your free Basic Account! With this account you have the following benefits:

- 100 responses per survey
- 10 questions per survey
- 15 question types to choose from
- Ability to collect emails via weblink or email

Get started by checking out our online tutorials to learn how to use SurveyMonkey: http://www.surveymonkey.com/Home_Videos.aspx

If you need more advanced features, check out our Professional Account. For a low monthly fee of $19.95, a Professional Account provides you with:

- Unlimited number of responses*
- Unlimited questions per survey
- Ability to download responses into a spreadsheet
- Advanced reporting and charting tools
- Unlimited custom survey themes
- Create skip logic

To view all of the benefits of a Professional Account visit: http://www.surveymonkey.com/Home_Pricing.aspx

*Additional charges may apply for over 1000 responses a month (applies to monthly and quarterly subscriptions only)

If you need to contact us for any reason, please click the "Need Help?" button on the site. Through the Help Centre, you can contact our support staff and access a knowledgebase with hundreds of answers, online tutorials, and a downloadable user manual and survey design guide.

Regards,

SurveyMonkey Customer Service

School Marketing Plan Evaluation

The SMP needs to be evaluated at the end of each year.

Stakeholders

Representatives from the Key Stakeholders groups within the school need to give input.

These people would include:

- Principal and Leadership Team
- School Manager
- Parish Priest
- Staff (as decided in consultation with Principal)
- Parent representatives
- Student Leaders
- Feeder School Principals and Leadership Teams
- Media Representatives (usually media contacts of yours and advertising consultants you dealt with, as needed)
- Systemic representatives as needed

Survey and Feedback

Feedback quantity and quality will vary.

Requested replies would be from both specific and general groups, for example, you may target specific groups of Parents e.g. School Board, but also invite interested Parents through the schools' newsletters to respond.

A simple questionnaire sent to these people asking three questions will often give enough detail for a fair appraisal and follow-up discussion with the School leadership team and SMM.

You may be inclined to do this through an online survey. (See previous section of this chapter for examples.)

The questions could be:

- **The SMP for [School Name] for this year was successful in what ways?**
- **The SMP for [School Name] for this year was lacking in what ways?**
- **How would you suggest the SMP for [School Name] be adjusted for next year?**
- **Other comments**

The SMM would then summarize these responses in an honest way and present the views to the School's Leadership Team.

It is also good to include specific examples from each question from key people e.g.

- a feeder school Principal may be the only one who is aware of issues regarding visitations or school involvement in his / her school
- a feeder school secretary may be the only one aware of specific parental / staff issues she hears espoused in her main office;

It is important that this isn't lost in the summary.

> Others may like to develop a survey which ranks specific statements about the SMP from 5 to 1. The number of statements in the survey would need to be minimal to gain a good percentage of replies.

This type of survey would more than likely achieve a greater number of responses, yet the detail is limited. You may like to try a greater number of statements for groups or individuals you feel are more likely to respond.

You may also like to include a section for written responses to questions similar to the above three.

SMM Support

> It is important that the SMM is supported by all groups to continue on the successful way or make various changes to improve.

Most common changes are made each year in the approach and / or forms of marketing used in each subsequent year.

This is normal and leads to a more successful SMP each year.

Regional Marketing Plan

Combined marketing for individual regions could benefit each school in that region.

Overview

Each school needs its own SMP and the right to implement it free from outside interference.

However, each school could also benefit from a Regional Marketing Plan (RMP).

This plan may be one that encompasses all, or a selection of schools, within the region.

The Regional Marketing Plan would be a means of sharing ideas, costs and expertise.

The region's School Principals and SMMs should meet to plan the best approach, including budget, roles, timeline, branding, etc.

The stronger the overall regional group of schools is seen within that community,

the stronger each individual school is often seen.

There is strength in numbers.

Approaches could include emphasizing each school's strength within the region e.g. Sporting Excellence Program, The Arts, Pastoral / Social Justice Programs, Curriculum Successes.

Advantages

It also often happens that when a school, which is perceived as more popular by sections of the community, is part of the RMP, each school gains from that perception.

The perceived popular school would not lose from this exposure because of its initial strength, along with it being seen as part of a strong viable network of like-minded schools.

The regional approach needs to account for the special needs, successes and expertise of a region, and hence the schools within that region, for a more successful RMP in that region.

Caution

Even though this may appear to save financially, it takes away from the individual uniqueness of each school.

Marketing is often more successful when emphasizing a uniqueness.

School Marketing Internet Applications

including

Samples and Instructions

Screenshots and Weblinks

School Marketing
Internet Applications

including
Samples and Instructions - Screenshots and Weblinks

The internet provides so many school marketing opportunities that are:

- very contemporary
- popular with a significant and ever-increasing number of our school community
- ever-growing in possibilities
- often inexpensive or free
- fun!

The modern school needs to be actively involved with many of these internet opportunities, otherwise they will unnecessarily fall behind the interest level and communication methods of an ever-growing number of our students, staff and their families – with what could be serious ramifications for all concerned.

The CHALLENGE has been issued!

Headings

Website
Website Management Software Sample
RSS Feeds
SEOs
Blogs
Emails
e/i-Newsletters and e/i-Flyers
Social Networking Websites
Video Uploads
Chat Rooms
Skype

Website

The school website is one of the most important forms of marketing the school. It is often where school information is initially found, especially by families new to the area.

The website is often one of the first places that potential families, students and potential staff get an overall feel and basic appreciation of the potential for their involvement in school life.

Creating a Website - Background

Investigation in this area is critical.

The school will need expertise to create and then continually update a good website.

The initial construction of the website may come from school IT staff or other staff, systemic IT specialists, parents with special IT skills or from outside commercial consultants.

The continual updating would best be done within the School. In-servicing staff for making these updates would be money well spent.

An option, I have found very beneficial, follows.

Management Software

Another option is to have the website embedded in to management software which allows for management of the site. This takes the site beyond the static and into the realm of continual fluid development – Web 2.0.

The expense of this option is not considerable and with negotiation within the field a reasonable monthly cost would be expected. I would suggest speaking with trusted others in deciding on the businesses offering this support.

(See 'Website Management Software Sample' in this chapter for a specific example.)

This software allows for various detailed reports of website usage. It could include:

- the whereabouts in the world of visitors to your site
- number of webpages they visited
- the content viewed from webpages and applications they visited
- where they entered and exited the website
- who is exploring your site, through IP (Internet Protocol) addresses
- the browsers they used to link to your website
- any commercial activities you may have as part of your website, etc.

This allows for the non-IT expert to update the website regularly, from uploading photos, literature items, to adding webpages, blogs, galleries of photos and videos, etc.

There are numerous other capacities depending on the management software. See the right hand columns in the screenshots below for details available though the management software I use.

Always Interactive supplies my management software. Three such samples of my website's details are included and shown below at: http://www.alwaysinteractive.com/

Reproduction of all 'Always Interactive' web-screens in this e-book reproduced with permission of Always Interactive at http://www.alwaysinteractive.com/.

Geographic Locations and Viewing Numbers - below

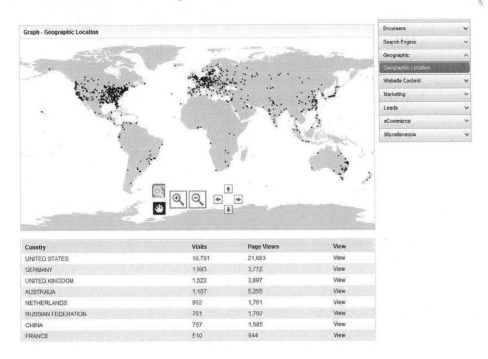

Country	Visits	Page Views	View
UNITED STATES	10,791	21,683	View
GERMANY	1,993	3,772	View
UNITED KINGDOM	1,522	3,897	View
AUSTRALIA	1,107	5,255	View
NETHERLANDS	962	1,751	View
RUSSIAN FEDERATION	761	1,702	View
CHINA	707	1,585	View
FRANCE	510	944	View

Webpages Viewed and Numbers per Page - below

Search Engine Transfers to SMA website - below

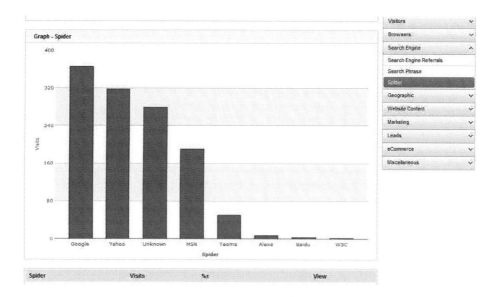

Target Audiences

The website is also where more and more students and parents will continually visit throughout their time in the school.

School Marketing Managers and key school staff should use the website for interaction between the various stakeholders within the school e.g. their students, potential students, staff, families and other interested people including parishioners.

Regularly updated bulletin boards and newsletters, upcoming liturgical and social events, St Vincent de Paul and other charitable needs and requests, photo and video galleries of school activities, etc, are needed.

Website Examples

To view good school websites, for ideas for your own school's website, just go to your browser and type in such words as: 'outstanding school websites', 'school websites', 'best school websites', etc. There are so many good examples out there.

You may also visit various school websites, system-level office websites and diocesan websites for both ideas and for key personnel.

Below are three good examples. St Joseph's Hunters Hill and Brisbane Catholic Education sites see the News as central to their homepage. Another similar site worth viewing is the Loreto Toorak site at: http://www.loretotoorak.vic.edu.au/home/.

The following is reproduced with permission of St Joseph's College, Hunters Hill and may be found at: http://www.joeys.org/index.cfm

The BCE homepage is produced with permission of Brisbane Catholic Education and is found at: http://www.bne.catholic.edu.au/

Another often used style for homepages emphasizes detail. It is very important that it is presented in an attractive, clear and succinct format. A good example of an archdiocesan website is included with permission from the Archdiocese of Brisbane and found at http://bne.catholic.net.au/asp/index.asp

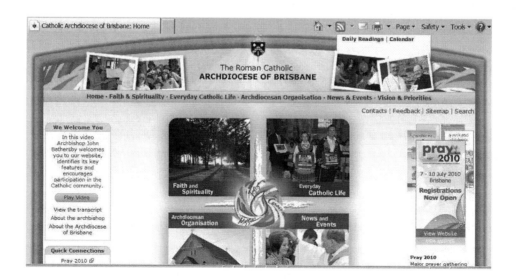

Another good example follows and is reproduced with permission of Saint Ignatius College, Riverview http://www.riverview.nsw.edu.au/

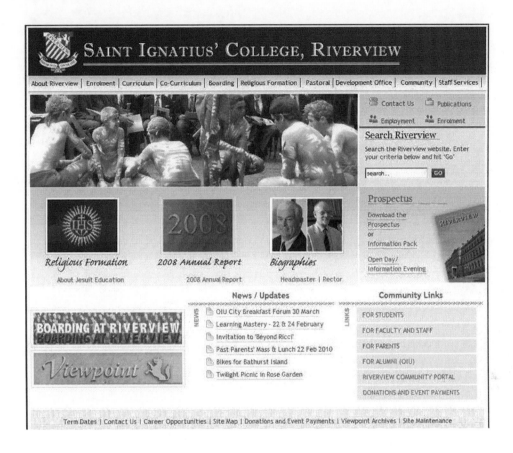

Website Inclusions

Many good ideas can be gained from exploring the World Wide Web (WWW or Web or Internet) and noting characteristics that may be included on your website.

This exploration would be relevant both for those about to create a website and those who are / will be doing the updating.

Homepage

The homepage is the most important page to get correct. It is the page the viewer normally reaches on their initial search. First impressions are critical.

The appearance needs to be in-line with the school's selected branding styles:

- colors
- photos (for ease of acquiring and using professional images, check out such sites as: istockphoto (http://www.istockphoto.com/index.php) and crestock.com (http://www.crestock.com/). These sites provide professional standard images at relatively inexpensive rates. You buy royalty-free images which you can then use on your website. You may, however, have good professional ones done for you. These photos need to be professionally presented. Don't skimp on costs here.)
- logo
- motto or catchphrase
- selected key words and key phrases
- good graphics
- clear, directing toolbar/s and other links
- attention grabbing inclusions e.g.
    * news updates
    * upcoming events
    • webpages on your website listed

- **School - Parish Weblinks**

Another good sample of a homepage is included with permission from The Catholic Parish of Southport and shown here and found at: http://scp.org.au/.

Religious schools should have weblinks with their parish/es.

This allows for visitors to the church website to see the schools within the parish. It also allows for visitors to the school website to see links with their parish.

Both groups would benefit from this obviously stated link.

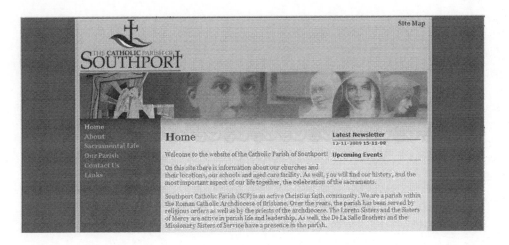

Clicking on 'About Us' takes you to the Parish Schools details at:
http://scp.org.au/parish_contacts.php

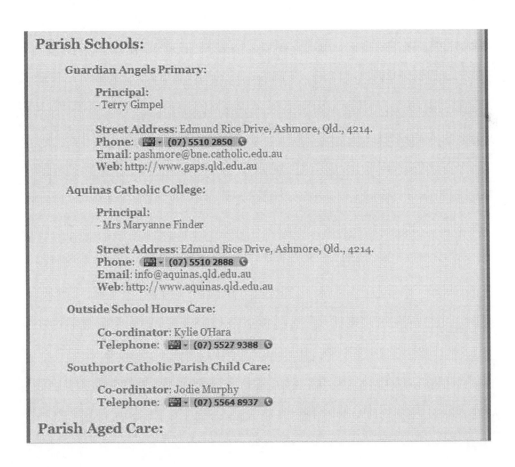

The Toolbar needs your website's important categories displayed clearly and efficiently. Areas would usually include a number of the following:

- Home
- About Us
- News
- Information for Students
- Information for Staff
- Information for Parents, including Enrolment details and Prospectus, etc
- Past Students
- Newsletter
- Photo and Video Galleries
- Search option
- Contact Details
- Connection for Staff and Students (to the school network for emails and other network options, including assessment tasks, weblinks, etc, if available)

Webpage Templates

Templates for each additional webpage, following the Homepage, should be similar in appearance but allowing for the specialty of each page.

If the website has a blog, the Blog page would need specific inclusions not on any other page e.g. 'Recent Posts', 'Archive' and 'Tags'. (More Blogging details follow shortly.)

Your exploration of good websites on the internet will help with your decisions. As styles develop, quality improves and fashions appear, your internet searches for good sites and their inclusions will be of significance to your final website templates.

Keep you website feeling FRESH.

Other Inclusions

These should be added as soon as possible, allowing for budget restraints, interests of the users / potential users and expertise of web-builders and web-managers:

- **Blogs** – these are becoming quite common amongst many staff, students and parents, so the use of these would be considered important by many people.

  Blogs allow for interaction of website viewers with your site. Blogs are posted and people interact either by just viewing what was written or by adding their own

thoughts. You have the capacity to allow all comments sent or only the selected comments you would like being viewed by your website's audience.
(See more on Blogs later.)

A sample introduction to a blog taken from the SMP website follows. The complete Blog Post (contents of this photo) may be found at:
http://www.schoolmarketingaustralia.com/ blog/School Marketing Blog/post/ School Marketing Plan Refreshed for 2010/

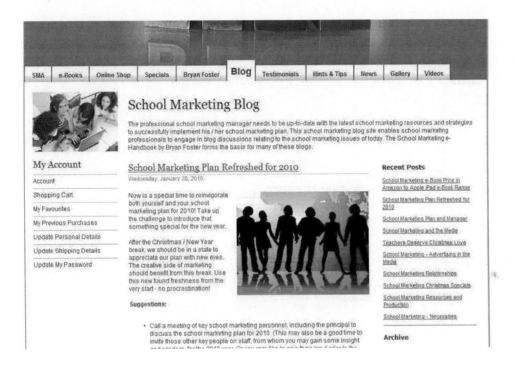

There are also many commercially available and free to operate blogs. These will allow you to say whatever you like in varying lengths from quite substantial down to a rather restricted 140 words on Twitter.

Twitter is a rather interesting and very quickly growing mini blog.

(More details on Twitter later.)

At this stage an example page is reproduced with permission from Twitter, Inc. and found at my home page at http://twitter.com/home

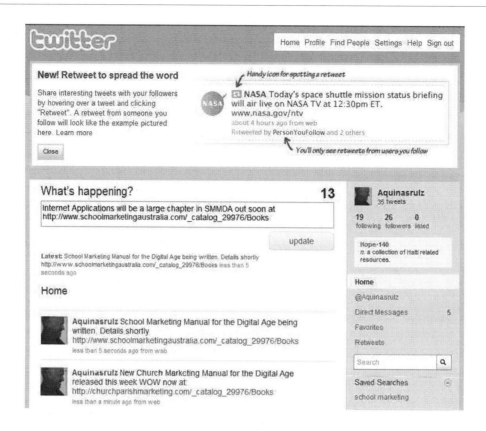

- **Photo Galleries** and **Video Galleries** are also seen by many as a necessary part of any good website. Schools should include a selection of school activities and involved students representing a cross section of these activities and demographics.

A Photo Gallery sample is shown below. I use a SMAPL one so as support the privacy of students and staff at school website galleries.
http://www.schoolmarketingaustralia.com/_webapp_273927/Marketing_the_School_'Always'

Interestingly, people enjoy either very geometric photo presentations, such as squares, whereas I personally enjoy the presentation fitting each actual photo. You can easily make all photos fit a certain geometric square in most cases by making sure each is sized to a predetermined measurement.

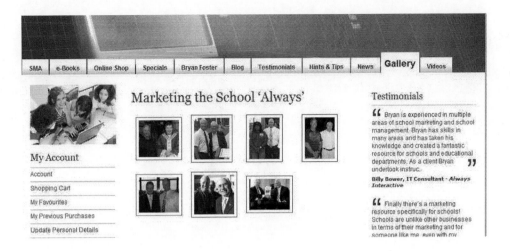

- **'You Tube'** videos being embedded into your website also adds another dimension to your website. Once again, you have full control over what you add.

Once the School Web Manager appreciates the management software then embedding 'You Tube' into the site's HTML is usually a simple task.

The sample below may be found embedded in the SMP website at:
http://www.schoolmarketingaustralia.com/

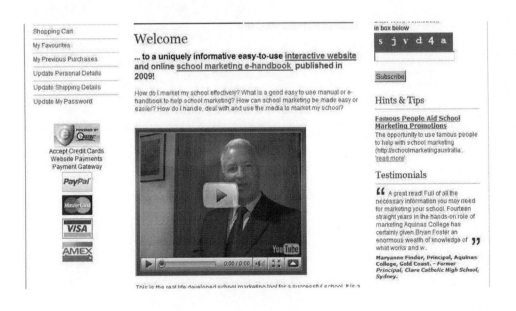

(More on 'You Tube' later.)

- **Podcasts** - audio and video recordings highlighting key aspects of the school life, would be added to the school website as needed. This is a different approach to embedding 'You Tube' videos or audios. Your web-builder, or technical staff expert, would most likely need to assist you with this embedding. (In addition to Podcasts see more on the School DVD / CD later in this e-book.)

  An Archdiocesan Podcast sample has been included with permission from the Archdiocese of Brisbane and may be found at:

  http://bne.catholic.net.au/asp/index.asp And click on 'Play Video' in left column.

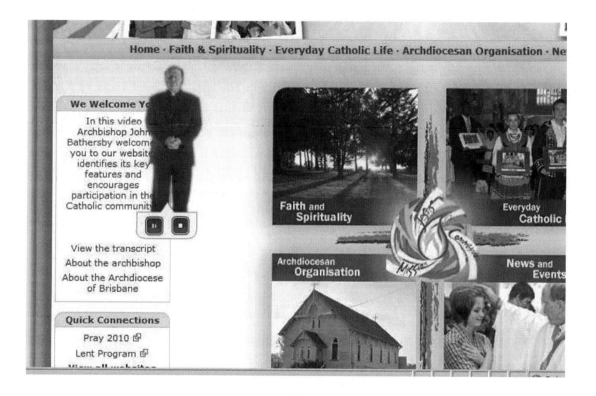

- **Social Networking** sites such as **'Facebook', 'myspace', 'LinkedIn' and 'Twitter'**, etc are also becoming the norm for many in the school community. Schools will need to consider including these links to and from the school website in their marketing plan.

  That is, if you decide to go ahead with this, you will need to develop a school profile and / or school principal / leader profile, or other key personnel within the school profiles, etc. at these various social networking websites and then link your website to these pages either through links or through RSS feeds.

(More about Social Networking and RSS feeds later in this chapter.)

You may also link from the social networking sites back to your school website. Generally for schools, I would recommend both directional links.

Domain Names / URLs

Each website has a unique Domain Name / URL (Uniform Resource Locator). These may be purchased from a number of suppliers. Just search 'Domain Names' in your search engine and a large selection of suppliers will be found.

Most schools would be either be linked off their institutional website, or create their own website and hence have a unique school domain name, or have both.

You can have numerous domain names linked to your one website. This means that each time a person types any domain name linked to your website into the top URL bar of their browser the visitor would end up on your website. Most major sites only need one domain name; however others may be purchased to avoid any confusion with other institutions with similar names.

It may also be advisable to purchase similar names with key words changed to avoid confusion with other similar school names.

Schools would normally purchase .edu domains.

However, as most people are so used to using .com, it may be advisable to also include this domain as well. Hence, if visitors type your domain with a .com they would be transferred to the correct website.

Legal Advice

You will need to also include legal statements explaining your conditions and terms of use for visitors to your website.

Statements such as on:

- Copyright
- Privacy Policy
- Web Disclaimer
- Conditions of Use
- Blog Conditions of Use

Most major school organizations these days would have their umbrella organization offering suggestions for these inclusions.

Otherwise, I would suggest seeking your own legal advice.

Website Creation, Hosting and Costs

- **Overview**

> Websites can be as simple as a few basic pages through to highly sophisticated fully interactive commercial sites.

Costs for creating the site and hosting it vary according to your selected approach. There are even free or inexpensive ways of gaining a website.

Beware of the free approaches, in case there are catches / issues of which you may not be aware. Remember that when you pay anything, or agree to their terms and conditions, you will be a part of some sort of contract – important to read the fine print.

- **Commercial website build and hosting**

If it was decided to go through a normal website creation business to build and host your website be prepared to pay anything from a few thousand to tens of thousands of dollars for the website build, depending on complexity + monthly hosting charges often between $50 and $100 (as at time of writing).

- **School, System or Institute Web-Builders**

> Many schools would use their system's / institution's experts or even qualified experts on the school staff.
> In secondary school there could be students capable of doing a reasonable creation.

These options offer more peace of mind, someone to contact to meet the website adjustment / changes requirements and to answer or solve my difficulties. They also take responsibility for system breakdowns, etc.

Good companies / systems / institutes should also have an educational component for the school, which is very beneficial for ongoing improvements and additions to the website.

- **School Website Needs**

Firstly decide what you need:

> * the purpose of your school website
> * allocated budget (this can grow in time, once confidence and availability of funds increases, etc. Best to start small than not start at all!)
> * who does the creativity overview / graphics / photos used / website design and who will build your site (saves money if someone in-house at your school / system / institution does as much as possible) – quotes and appreciation of services offered are needed
> * who will oversee the whole process and keep in constant contact with web designers, which could take some time depending on the complexity
> • am I fully aware of all the implications, especially if deciding on a cheap alternative?

- **Best Website Building and Hosting Approach for Your School?**

> * Decide on the best approach for your school. The three main options for most schools are:
>
> > • School pays for development and website hosting and usually gets own domain name.
> > • School links with other schools / system / institution to share development and housing costs. Each school has its own webpages as part of a larger website. The school name would usually be an extension of the larger group's domain name.
> > • School initially decides on a free or inexpensive website linked to major commercial blog websites. (See Inexpensive or Free Websites with Samples chapter.)

Inexpensive or Free Websites with Samples

I mention two other options which may be worth considering. These are two growth areas for relatively inexpensive websites.

Research Needed

I recommend you do your own research for these options and discuss with others the various implications each offers and whether either is worth pursuing for your school. Read the Terms and Conditions carefully. Following is an overview and samples for various options.

Online Web Hosting and Web Creating Services

- Online web hosting and web creating services can be relatively inexpensive. Here you develop your own website following their instructions. Your site can offer the basics through to the commercial. I would tend toward the more well known companies until my experience was more complete and I appreciated the numerous options and possible pitfalls certain businesses may offer.

  One example you could explore is at Yahoo http://smallbusiness.yahoo.com/

Blogs as Websites

- Blogs as websites.

  You can develop various commercially owned blog sites into your own school de-facto website, sometimes for free. It will be linked to the blogsite's domain usually e.g. http://schoolmarketingmanual.wordpress.com/

  For a fee you can add much more than the basics offered for free. This may include your own domain / URL name, as well as designing the layout more to your style - adding various widgets such as RSS feeds, calendars, etc. All but the basics will cost a fee.

See WordPress for examples of what is **free** with them at
http://en.wordpress.com/features/
and for a **fee** at http://en.wordpress.com/products/.
You may be pleasantly surprised.

It is also interesting to see which companies use this blogsite. Links to examples are at the 'Features' weblink above. One such example at time of writing is CNN Political Ticker Blog at
http://politicalticker.blogs.cnn.com/?fbid=C66PNrCE1OH

> Small and non-affluent schools may find this as a temporary means
> for having a free / inexpensive website.
> The expense increases with additions.

WordPress Samples

I will show a possibility of using a free blog I set up through WordPress, as an example. For interest I have created a four page website.

> This free blog even includes an embedded You Tube video (see 'Uploading Videos' in chapter), logo and photos.

The Blog has been called 'School Marketing Manual'. It contains some information from my SMP website at http://marketschools.com/
This blog has been reproduced with permission from WordPress at http://wordpress.com/

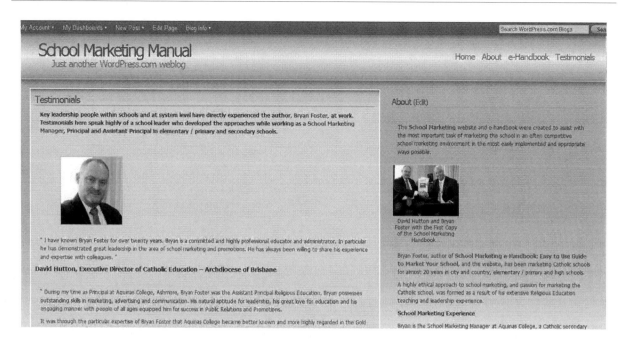

The blog is on one of many free templates from WordPress. This one is called - Andreas04.

I will add a couple of other samples to show how the same text and images may appear when placed in different templates. The next templates are known as:
INove and MistyLook.

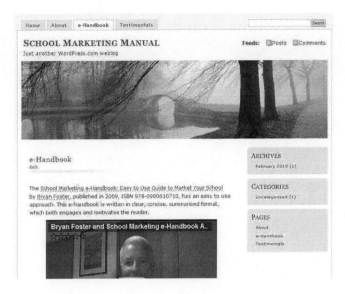

Google's Examples

Google also offers a free blog service. I have included the first page you would go to with Google to create this site. You will need to have a Google account before beginning the website creation journey. Just follow the prompts to create the website.

https://www.google.com/accounts/ServiceLogin?continue=https%3A%2F%2Fsites.google.com%2Fsite%2F&followup=https%3A%2F%2Fsites.google.com%2Fsite%2F&service=jotspot&ul=1

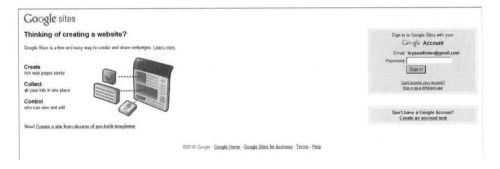

A sample of a free Google website follows. I have not added any other detail other than the site's name so that you can see how it looks once you have decided on the particular template you would like to use. You are then invited to learn all that is required to create your website through various links emanating from this page.

https://sites.google.com/site/schoolmarketingmanual/

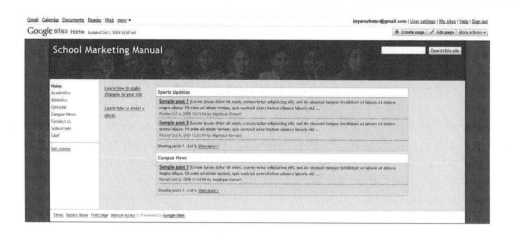

CAUTION

Be careful to understand the Terms and Conditions for these blogsites.
You would need to know if they can delete your blogsite and hence your school site without warning, etc.
I would suggest that these may be impermanent additions for your school.
You never know when terms and conditions may change!
However, for a fee the security of tenure increases.

Website Management
Software Sample

As an example of this sort of software, which I find enormously helpful for website administration and my 'online business / website' evaluation, etc,
let us explore a program called Iceberg

An informative introductory slideshow about the Iceberg software, which I have reproduced below with permission from 'Always Interactive', may be found at: http://www.alwaysinteractive.com/iceberg/quicktour/

You may also be interested in an introductory video which may be found at http://www.alwaysinteractive.com/iceberg/video/

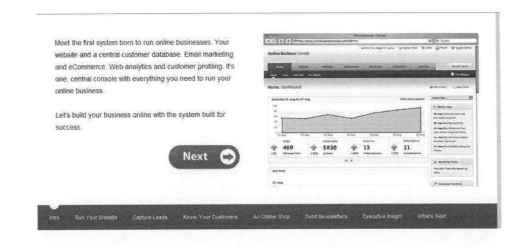

Run your website

The system will host your website and enable YOU to manage it without a programmer.

Beyond web pages, you can create a community with forums, build an audience with blogs, make secure areas for VIP content... and more.

Next ➡

Intro   Run Your Website   Capture Leads   Know Your Customers   An Online Shop   Send Newsletters   Executive Insight   What's Next

Capture leads

React faster - build smart web forms that notify you instantly by email and SMS when you get a new customer!

You can use a point-n-click approach to build custom web forms that capture every inquiry in a contact managment database, so you'll never lose a lead.

Next ➡

Intro   Run Your Website   Capture Leads   Know Your Customers   An Online Shop   Send Newsletters   Executive Insight   What's Next

Know your customers

With your online business console, every web inquiry, every purchase and every action is being recorded against a customer record.

Over time you'll get a complete picture of every customer and how they interact with your business, all from your built-in contact database.

Next ➡

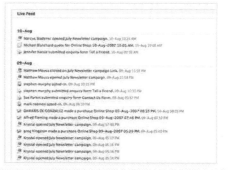

Intro   Run Your Website   Capture Leads   Know Your Customers   An Online Shop   Send Newsletters   Executive Insight   What's Next

An online shop

Set up an online shop and sell your products in a matter of minutes with your online business' online shop management features.

Without extra software, without extra effort you can sell products, fulfill orders, manage stock levels and collect payments automatically.

Next ➡

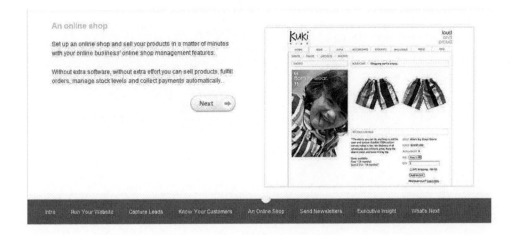

Intro   Run Your Website   Capture Leads   Know Your Customers   An Online Shop   Send Newsletters   Executive Insight   What's Next

Send newsletters

Email marketing is the most effective form of marketing available to a business owner.

With your online business console, you can send newsletters and other campaigns to targeted lists of customers that you've saved in Online Business Console' built-in contact database.

Next ➡

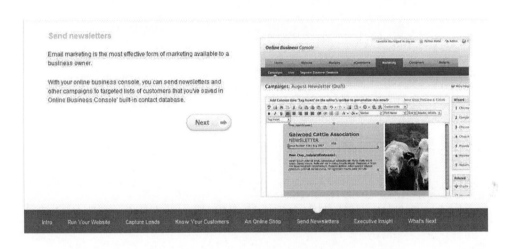

Intro   Run Your Website   Capture Leads   Know Your Customers   An Online Shop   Send Newsletters   Executive Insight   What's Next

Executive insight

Log in, and you're greeted with an instant overview of how your business is tracking from 4 key metrics.

From there you can drill down into detailed reports on your website, marketing campaigns and e-commerce performance.

Next ➡

Intro   Run Your Website   Capture Leads   Know Your Customers   An Online Shop   Send Newsletters   Executive Insight   What's Next

Once you begin using software such as this, you should have available to you from the supplier considerable 'help desk' assistance. This Iceberg program does. If other management software you are considering does not, I would suggest seriously considering your options.

RSS Feeds

RSS (Really Simple Syndication) feeds allow for your website visitors to register to receive updates you make to selected webpages which have this additional RSS capacity.

Advantages of RSS

Active websites are continually updating the information available to visitors to their sites. To make it as simple as possible for interested visitors to receive your updated information, you could make various webpages on your website RSS feed active i.e. if people register for receiving your updates they will receive these as your updates become available.

For schools the most likely RSS activation would be for their:

- e-newsletter
- news
- blog pages.

In time you would become aware of which pages you continually update and hence would be of interest to the school community and other interested people. These could then be added to the RSS list.

Simple methods are shown below for:

- creating RSS feeds on your website and
- receiving selected RSS feeds.

Symbols

or RSS are common RSS feed symbols appearing on most websites and found at http://www.microsoft.com/technet/security .

Sample Website with RSS facility

For a sample website look at http://marketschools.com/ .

On this website pages offering this facility are:

- Blogs
- News
- Hints and Tips
- Specials

However, you may link virtually as many of your website's webpages through RSS Feeds as you desire, as long as your website's management system has the capacity.

School Website Developers adding RSS Feeds

Good website management software has the capacity to add RSS links for your web-pages. This should be a simple procedure.

An example is from the SMP website. Here we use the Iceberg management software from Always Interactive as shown below and available at http://www.alwaysinteractive.com/

Only four fields need to be completed before pressing 'Save':

- RSS Channel Name
- Update Frequency
- RSS Channel Description
- Enable (for page to go live)

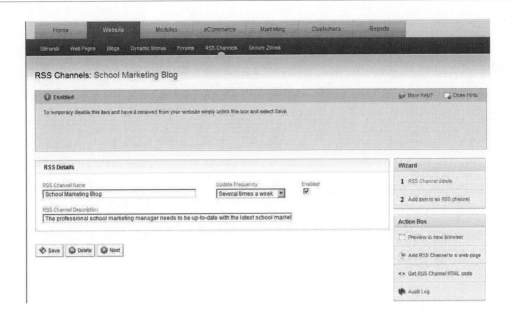

There are many websites which have various offers for adding RSS feeds to your website. A quick search of your search engines will show the many options worth exploring. Use terms such as 'adding RSS feed to website' for best results.

Once again, I very much favor the software management option.

Visitors Subscribing to a RSS Feed

1. Click the RSS feeds symbol, e.g. 🔊, on the page where the symbol occurs: either on the webpage itself or on the browser toolbar with that page
2. Click 'Subscribe to this Feed'
3. Give the feed a title
4. Select the folder for the feed
5. Click 'Subscribe'

RSS Symbol Location for a Webpage

The RSS symbol will usually appear in color when active either on the:

- browser's toolbar of the page offering RSS feeds or
- webpage itself which is offering the RSS feed.

Sample RSS Feed

An example of an RSS feed from the SMP website follows.

Click on the orange RSS feed symbol on the toolbar of the browser at on this following screen.

This webpage below then appears at
http://marketschools.com/RSSRetrieve.aspx?ID=2480&Type=RSS20

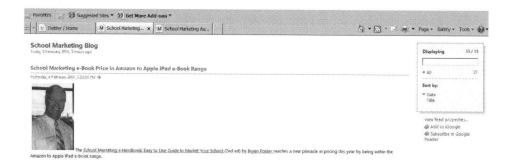

Follow the prompts as you make your selections from the screen above.

When you click on 'Subscribe to this feed' on your browser on the above screen, you will go to http://marketschools.com/RSSRetrieve.aspx?ID=2480&Type=RSS20, which is shown below.

Click on Subscribe and you are then registered. This now becomes a part of the 'Favorites' section in your browser. To view this RSS feed click on the Favorites key on your browser. In the following screen it is in the top left corner. For this example you will see the following at the above URL.

RSS Symbol Different Location

If we looked at the 'News' page on the SMP website, we would find the RSS symbol on the webpage itself – just above the beginning of the News' article. We would click on this to subscribe and make the appropriate selections.
(See http://marketschools.com/news)

Viewing RSS Feeds

- 'Favorites' - To view these RSS feeds created in your 'Favorites', all you need to do is click on the 'Favorites' button on your browser toolbar, select 'Feeds' tab and there are the Feeds.
- 'iGoogle' or 'Google Reader' - Another popular option for the placement of the feeds is at Google - going to 'iGoogle' or 'Google Reader'. All you need to do is select either of these options in that first selection box above. You will need to register for these options separately though.
- Other options also exist. See Microsoft link below as an example.

RSS Feeds Further Explained

You will also notice in two screens above that when you click on the 'Learn more about feeds' blue link the right hand column called 'Using feeds (RSS)' appears. Follow this column down for a good explanation of the FAQs (Frequently Asked Questions) about RSS feeds.

Another professional presentation, including other options, is done by Microsoft and may be found at http://www.microsoft.com/technet/security

Further explanations of RSS are also available from various websites – just search through your browsers.

Search Engine Optimization (SEO) for School Websites

To gain higher positioning at various search engines such as Google, Yahoo, You Tube, Bing, Baidu (China) and AOL Search, etc various methods of SEO are needed.

Website Viewers

Some schools aren't really interested in having their website visited from people all over the world. These school communities are more interested in their local communities. For these people SEOs are not needed.

Various communities might like their website to be easily accessible to people from various parts of their particular country but not necessarily beyond their borders. This allows for people transferring to their school to preview what the school has to offer. A suggestion for these communities would be to select a domain name which ends in their countries code e.g. United Kingdom .uk, for Australia .au, etc.

Other communities may be interested in having their school and their website open worldwide. SEOs would likely suit these schools.

Top Search Engine Page is the Aim

The aim with SEO is to achieve in the top three on the first page of any search engine. The following example from Google shows School Marketing Australia, publisher of this e-book, at #3 on page 1 of the worldwide search for School Marketing. Found at: http://www.google.com.au/#hl=en&source=hp&q=school+marketing&meta=&aq=f&oq=school+marketing&fp=117628ddce3be56e

The charged 'Sponsored Links' whereby companies pay to have their advert placed on this page are in the right hand column, while the 278 000 000 sites relying on SEO are in the main left column.

Suggestions for Improvement

Some ways I have found which I believe help with Search Engine Optimization are:

- The **Domain name** includes the school name and suburb.
- **Key Words** such as the school name are regularly used throughout the site, particularly in titles / headings, first sentence and last sentence on each webpage.
- Each webpage within the website would highlight something different about the school and hence also include **other key words** associated both with the school name / suburb and that webpage's emphasis.

  These other Key Words may be: principal, school staff, curriculum, religious education, contact us, priests, open day, prospectus, sporting / arts / welfare etc groups within the school, etc.

  The key would for impact could have the school name before it e.g. aquinas college principal. This links the purpose of the webpage specifically with the school.
- Each **Blog Post's** title, along with the first and last sentences would include key words associated with that individual blog's message and that it eventuated from your school.
- The more **links coming to your website** from other sources, particularly **.gov, .edu and .org** the better. Having other sites point to your website helps SEO i.e. having other sites have your Domain / URL linked live on their website.

  However, it is best not to swap links with others of similar level e.g. .org. That is, if each site has the other's site linked from their site, this usually causes it to neutralize the impact for both sites.

  Yet swapping these links may **improve traffic to your site**, just not higher SEO.

- Include **links within your own site** to various other webpages on your site.
- Another way of achieving the links from other sites may be achieved by developing various **Blogs elsewhere** which include the link to your website. (More on this in Blogs later.)
- **Be careful not to overdo all these links and key words as search engines may penalize you for being overambitious in gaining notice for your website.**
- **Age of the website**. Older sites have more credibility. Develop your website as soon as possible.
- **Update your site** regularly. A fresh, updated site is appealing to both visitors and for SEO.
- **Paid Ads** will gain you high positioning in the 'Sponsored' columns, but at a cost, usually on a pay per click per view system. This may be quite expensive for a school's needs.

Blogs

This is becoming a very popular form of interactive, digital communication by internet users.
Content may be brief or extensive.

Explained

Blogs are used to allow interaction between the website's administrator/s and the website's visitors.

Schools could benefit considerably through the effective use of Blogs. These are ideal avenues to promote your school and the various messages you wish to place in the public or private domain.

These days so many people wish to be valued through their involvement and feedback - blogs are one highly regarded avenue for them to achieve this.

Blog Posts

The website's / blog's administrators write a Blog Post (comment, information, news, challenge, etc.) and publish this to their website's blog page. Blog Posts may also include photos, videos, audios and other graphic presentations.

The visitor to your website's blog page would then have the option to comment on your blog post's content.

Blog Posts may be of any length and literary style depending on the target audience. However, in most cases, brevity is the norm in these days of mass communication overload. Think newspaper article lengths for most blog posts. As a general guide I work on 200-300 words per blog post. 300 words is often quoted for a good SEO.

You need to make sure that the administrator has the option to accept or reject all comments posted in response to the blog post. If the blog post is available to the public, you need to be prepared to receive all sorts of comments, including spam (mainly advertising links). Unsuitable comments would then be deleted.

Two Major Blog Uses for Schools

School Marketers could use blogs in two primary ways:

- School website Blog
- External Blog sites, which you would point (link) back to your school website.

School Website's Blog

The school website would include a Blog page. On this page there would be the blog posts listed in sequential order with the most recent placed at the top of the page.

The Blog Page would also normally include: 'Recent Posts', an 'Archive' of previous blog posts and previous 'Tags' (key words used to attract attention to each specific blog post).

It is important to also include 'Blog Condition of Use' details on your website. An example of one may be found at:

http://marketschools.com/blog-conditions-of-use

Legal advice should be sort to ascertain your particular needs.

A Sample Blog Page is at: http://marketschools.com/ blog/School_Marketing_Blog

The creation of this blog post follows.

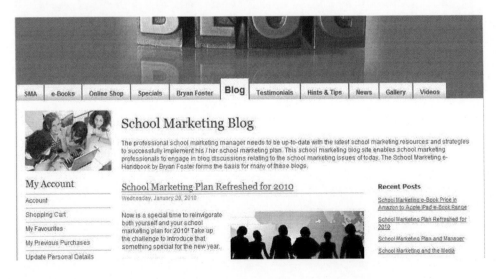

Management Software

To administer the Blog page, as for all the other webpages, etc on the school website, you will need either a good appreciation of website building software or access to reasonably simple management software to achieve the task. I use Iceberg (Business Catalyst) through Always Interactive at: http://alwaysinteractive.com/

The example below shows one such blog post's administration page. This is where you complete the details for each blog post, including the:

- Title
- Release Date
- Tags
- Blog Content.

You can insert:

- photos
- videos
- tables
- various web links etc.

There are also a large variety of other options for the presentation e.g. color, fonts, letter size, wrap-around, etc.

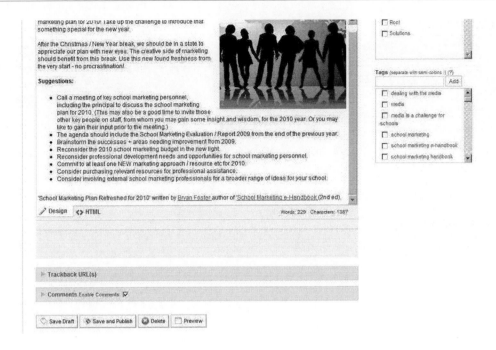

External Blog Sites

The external blog site could be used for three main reasons:

- these increase traffic to your School website through the links you include in the general blog template you create, and also in the blog posts you write, which are directed to your School's website
- these assist with your website's SEO (Search Engine Optimization) as each point (links, as per above) back to your School website assists the SEO
- in most cases these external blogs are free of charge.
  (Costs are optional depending on your usage and blog complexities and on the Blog provider. In most cases you can easily do this free of charge.)

A good example of these external blogs are provided by **Blogger and WordPress**.

Following is an example of both the Blogs and Blogs Posts for Blogger. (WordPress Blog examples are shown in 'Website Creation, Hosting and Costs' section previously.) There is also information to start the development of Blogger and WordPress blogs.

Also included are domain listings for other popular external blog sites.

Blogger and How to Join

Blogger Homepage may be found at: http://www.blogger.com/start
An example of a Blogger Blog may be found at: http://marketschools.blogspot.com/

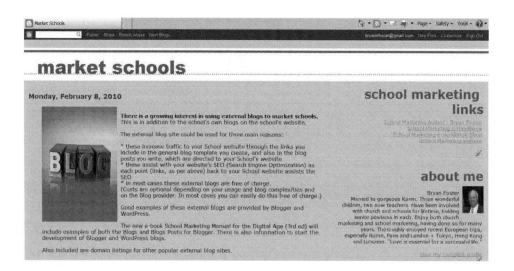

To create a Blogger Account you first of all need to create a Google Account as Blogger belongs to Google. You then follow the 'Continue' key to create the Blogger Account.

To create a Blogger Account go to: https://www.blogger.com/start. Initially click on 'Create a Blog'.

(Images of the web pages you need to complete online follow.)

The page below will then appear at: https://www.google.com/accounts/NewAccount?service=blogger&continue=https%3A%2F%2Fwww.blogger.com%2Floginz%3Fd%3D%252Fcreate-blog

Click on 'Continue' to go to next page for 'Name your blog': http://www.blogger.com/
create-blog.g?pli=1

The new Blogger account and new blog naming process is now complete.

All you need to do now is select the template (how your blog will appear)

http://www.blogger.com/choose-template

and then start putting in as much, or as little, detail you so desire about your school and / or self and then begin blogging… Enjoy!

Other External Blogs

- **WordPress**
  The WordPress Homepage can be found at: http://wordpress.com/

Webpages below reproduced with permission of WordPress.

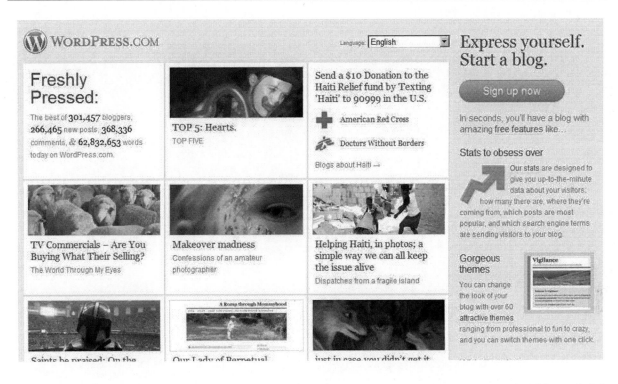

To create a WordPress Account click on the 'Sign up now' button on the right hand side and go to: http://en.wordpress.com/signup/ From their just follow the instructions and form your own Blog.

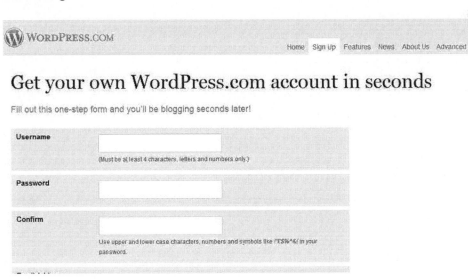

- **Squarespace**

   This is relatively new to the blogging scene with numerous outstanding features. Costs from $US8 to $US50 per month at time of writing. Worth a look. Very impressive reviews from the Wall Street Journal Online and CNET Webware. http://www. squarespace.com/

- **TypePad**

  TypePad was launched in 2003 and has been used by major corporations such as BBC – quite a broad spread of users. Found at: http://www.typepad.com/pro/#2 Costs from $US8.95 to $US89.95 per month at time of writing.

- Other common blogs are available at:

  http://www.joomla.org/
  http://www.movabletype.org/
  http://www.tumblr.com/
  http://www.vox.com/

Conclusion

Numerous other examples of various blogs may also be found in the "Inexpensive or Free Websites with Samples' section earlier in this e-book.

The Blogger World is an exciting and often time consuming pastime or profession…

There are so many uses both from the school marketing perspective as well as a personal perspective. Personally I have developed the two Blogs on my official websites at:

School Marketing Blog site
School Marketing Blog site

as well as a number of Blogs, some of these you will see linked in this e-book:

Blogger
WordPress
LinkedIn (some of these you would have seen linked in this chapter).

Once you begin on the Blogging path you will find so many uses, particularly in being able to espouse your viewpoints to the world! And have people throughout the world respond!

Email

Stakeholders within the school, especially staff, parents and students need to be encouraged to communicate by email when appropriate.

When used correctly, email is an efficient, quick form of written communication.

Considerable communication with commercial, pastoral and educational interests associated with the school will occur through email discussions / correspondence.

Protocols

Protocols of email usage should be followed.

Even though there appears to be growth occurring in these protocols, it would be fair to say that an email is virtually an electronic note or letter and should be treated as such.

It is not a text / txt message similar to use with a mobile / cell phone or a 'Twitter' comment (see 'Twitter' input later).

Correct language, grammar and punctuation are needed.

When it is sent at a professional level e.g. staff to staff, staff to parents and vice versa, professional writing protocols should be observed.

Staff Email

Staff emails need to be permanently configured so as to be based on a uniform template format which includes: Name, Title, School Address, Phone Number, Fax Number, Mobile / Cell Number and Skype Number, if appropriate, Email address and Web Address.

Other additions, such as a background, photo and qualifications may also be added.

Email Disclaimer

Also needed is a relevant disclaimer statement that follows all other detail. **An example is noted below:**

"Unless stated otherwise, this email, together with any attachments, is intended for the named recipient(s) only and may contain privileged and confidential information. If received in error, you are asked to inform the sender as quickly as possible and delete this email and any copies of this from your computer system network.

If not an intended recipient of this email, you must not copy, distribute or take any action(s) that relies on it; any form of disclosure, modification, distribution and/or publication of this email is also prohibited.

Unless stated otherwise, this email represents only the views of the sender and not the views of [School Name and Suburb etc]."

Staff should try and respond within the day to any emails, however this is not always possible and hence parents need to be aware of the busyness of school life and of school staff restrictions, and to make allowances for any delay.

Legal Advice

Legal or diocesan advice for any legal or similar type of statement on your email is recommended.

Email Challenges

When staff are responding to difficulties it is often best to approach these as challenges and to be treated with respect with the aim of getting a solution.

Emails should not take the place of interviews and telephone conversations when these others are the more appropriate form of communication.

Emails should not be used to hide behind!

Parents who believe they have gained a satisfactory result after such email/s and telephone call/s or interview/s often become the best marketing advocates for the school.

As they often say, "The School listens to me!"

Email Providers

There are a number of formats and providers for emails:

- You may choose to use software such as Windows Outlook operating on your computer and linking though your normal internet provider.
- You may choose this facility to be added to your own website in the form of a 'Contact Us' form, etc.
- A common format is the webmail available through various internet websites e.g. Google's Gmail and Yahoo's email, along with your internet provider's email.

Gmail welcome page may be found by clicking <u>Gmail</u>. It will appear as below.

(<u>https://www.google.com/accounts/ServiceLogin?service=mail&passive=true&rm=false&continue=https%3A%2F%2Fmail.google.com%2Fmail%2F%3Fui%3Dhtml%26zy%3Dl&bsv=zpwhtygjntrz&ss=1&scc=1&ltmpl=default&ltmplcache=2&hl=en</u>)

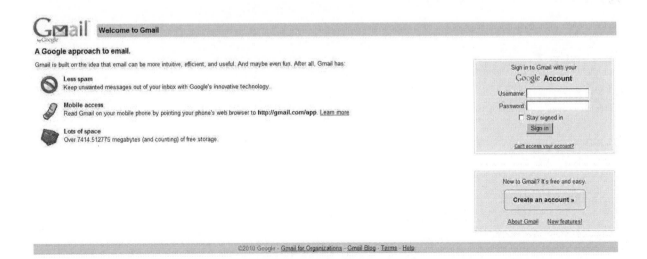

Yahoo Help (Sign-in and Registration) page is found at:

http://help.yahoo.com/l/us/yahoo/edit/

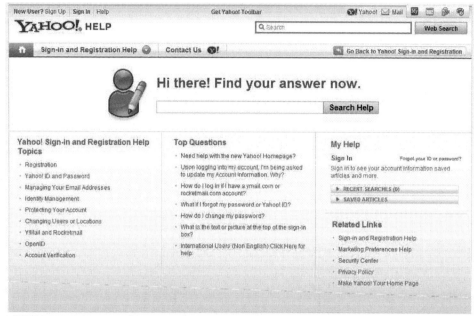

(Reproduced with permission of Yahoo! Inc. ©2010 Yahoo! Inc. YAHOO! and the YAHOO! logo are registered trademarks of Yahoo! Inc.)

e/i-Newsletter

The School Newsletter is often the best regular form of information-giving to Parents.
Either the
e-newsletter (sent out via email) or the
i-newsletter (placed on the school Internet website) or
both,
are popular in this digital age.

e-Newsletter / i-Newsletter + Newsletter - Essential

Both e-newsletter or i-newsletter will add to the target audience. That is, it is available for anyone requesting an email out from the school or to have the option of reading it on the school website.

Supplement these with the regular hardcopy available from the school for those in attendance or on a mail-out list and interested, or not interested in an e/i-newsletter, and the target base should be considerably more.

This section within this chapter will concentrate on the e-Newsletter / i-Newsletter. The hardcopy Newsletter will also be covered in the 'School Marketing Resources and Instructions' chapter.

Regular Weekly Publication

Regular weekly publication is needed for best success. **Regularity rules!**

The readership should often be expanded to neighboring / feeder schools and other interested schools and even to other willing sources e.g. parent and school businesses for display in reception rooms, offices, etc.

The school's website needs to be updated weekly with each e-newsletter uploaded to it. A collection of the year's i-newsletters on the website is appreciated by many Parents and others wanting to get an overview of the year's progress.

The e-newsletter would be either emailed to all interested parents and others as per a developed database and / or placed on the website as an i-newsletter. I would suggest both as people are more likely to read the email sent to them. Having the website archive as a backup helps considerably for people checking for previous e/i-newsletters / news, etc.

Professional e-Newsletter / i-Newsletter

A professional publication is needed.

The school's branding is very important and needs to be strategically positioned on the pages / website.

Photos 'tell a thousand words' and whenever possible should be used. Appropriate content, quality and sizing are essential for success.

This is especially true for an e/i-Newsletter where bright, interesting photos seem to 'often come to life' and add significantly to the effectiveness of the presentation. Hence the impact on the way in which each story is received by the reader.

The presentation can be quite outstanding when displayed on LCD monitors – use colors, text, images and layout wisely for maximum impact.

(However, paper copies should also be produced for presentation at the front office of the school and parish office.)

e-Newsletter / i-Newsletter Homepage +

Begin with the Homepage, usually written by the School Principal. Parents tend to read the points from the leader of the school first, and possibly only these. This homepage should include at least all the summarized main points from the e/i-newsletter.

The next page, or as the reader scrolls down, links to all the other articles.

When the link is clicked each of the articles appears on its own.

Production: In-house or Outsourced

The e/i-Newsletter may be produced through the school as either an emailed publication i.e. an attachment, or as an attached webpage to the school's websites.

Save as .pdf files before uploading or emailing-out.

The e-Newsletter may be outsourced to professional e/i-Newsletter producers. The firms usually don't charge much, however they require you to allow advertising by them on the e/i-Newsletter.

Sample e/i-Newsletter – Created by 'Schoolzine'

An example business is 'Always Interactive' which has a worldwide service, 'Schoolzine', available for schools and churches. To view the options go to their website at http://www.schoolzine.com.au/

"The majority of the production cost is subsidized by national companies and local businesses that pay 'Schoolzine' to advertise tastefully in the e-Newsletters. This allows schools to pay only a fraction of the cost. Only family friendly advertising is published in the e-newsletters and all with final approval from the school." (Schoolzine promotional literature)

The following screenshots are produced with permission of Always Interactive at http://www.alwaysinteractive.com/ who own 'Schoolzine'.
http://www.schoolzine.com.au/home.html & http://www.schoolzine.com.au/schools.html

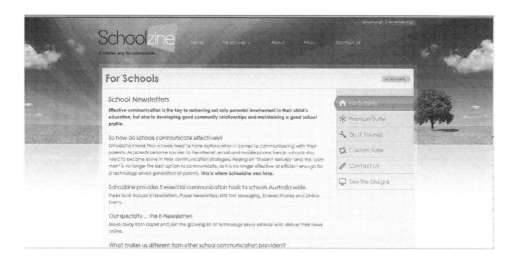

Sample e/i-Newsletter by 'Schoolzine' – Aquinas College

The Aquinas College s/i-newsletter is an example which uses 'Schoolzine'.

Below, reproduced with permission of Aquinas College, are two screenshots of their e/i-newsletter. The first is a segmented newsletter as it appears on arrival as an email attachment.

The second is a screenshot seen as you scroll down the e/i-newsletter to where the links to follow-up stories are located.

This following e/i-newsletter appeared at:
http://www.schoolzine.com.au/schools/A/aquinascollege/2010/20100129/

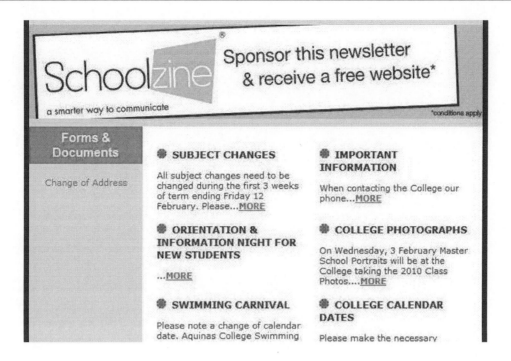

Effectiveness

It can be argued that most people read only the front page, which is usually written by the School Principal. If this is the case then the most important detail needs to be included here.

It follows that the newsletter's length be appropriate so that time and money is not wasted.

A good coverage of recent and upcoming events and activities, including a school and parish calendar, is the primary purpose of the newsletter.

Some form of weekly rotation of topics / staff or parents presenting articles may be needed for effectiveness. This would especially apply if there are many writers and topics to be covered. The Parish Priest should be included as regularly as possible.

Staff and parents should be encouraged to participate but according to certain parameters, especially length.

Brevity Rulz

> Brevity is once again paramount to these stories.
>
> This is often difficult for many people.
>
> These people need to be educated as to the best means of getting their information read in the newsletter.

Most importantly, staff and parent leaders need to feel valued for their input to the newsletter.

Advertising Dilemma

Many believe that the school should not be seen as a commercial enterprise but as a stand-alone educational institute.

They may also argue that advertisements aren't usually read, yet the placement can vary considerably due to the nature of webpages.

Electronic advertising is often more intrusive due to the high quality of the presentation and the special use of colors and design used to attract attention.

Advertisements need to be carefully selected so as to not impose on the overall production. The main purpose of the newsletter is not to advertise certain products.

When outsourced, schools need to be in philosophical alignment with the outsourced company's principles of advertising and the particular adverts used.

If the school can negotiate their own suppliers as advertisers, this should result in better success for the school, due to the often localized nature of the adverts i.e. supporting the local community and all the goodwill this generates.

The decision often comes down to the school's budgetary restraints.

Layout Development

Schools may have one or two staff that receive and do the newsletter's layout. This is good organizational practice.

If staff and parent leaders can electronically send their stories this improves the time taken and in a number of ways the effectiveness of the presentation. Electronic methods would be through the school's computer networks or as an email attachment.

This method should be considered essential for economy of time and expense reasons.

The attachments should include photos (+ captions explaining the photo, including the names of people from left to right) and directions to where photos are stored if on any server.

The School Principal, or designated staff member, would need to decide on specific articles for each week's publication. Some articles may need to be delayed in line with the rotation method of weekly article selection.

Proofing is essential!

e/i-Flyer

e-Flyers / i-Flyers are issued electronically whenever some important news or event is forthcoming.

When these appear on the school internet website the term i-Flyer is more accurate. Brevity and presentation is the secret.

Theme

A specific theme for each flyer needs to be apparent e.g. New School Principal, School Facility Opening, Curriculum Success, Major Arts / Sports Victories, Open Day, Parent Information Nights etc.

Other themes may be linked from the e/i-flyer, but best not to distract from the main theme. Most of the content and images visible should be based on the main theme.

Be aware that having a general themed flyer to promote the school will often say to the reader that the school needs more people.

Many people react against this.

Frequency

Due to the ease of production and success that these flyers invariably bring, it is **important not to overdo the frequency of email-outs and / or website postings**.

It would be hard to imagine the need for a frequency of less than fortnightly – so that the readers do not develop a blasé approach to the e/i-Flyers.

Purpose

The purpose is to inform the parents, potential families and other interested parties of the advantages of your school to the community through its ongoing prayer-life, communal activities and developments.

This should create a positive discussion. The prestige of the school should be raised or confirmed. Interest should be increased with potential new families to your school and school.

Distribution Methods

There are two main ways to distribute the flyers:

- e-Flyers are emailed: from school or third party production
- i-Flyer on the school internet website.

Email-outs

The e-flyer is either sent out directly via email attachment from the school or is sent via a third party who publishes the e-flyer for you.

It is best to then to also place the e-flyer on your school website.

Its placement on the website would depend on how you have decided to name your webpages e.g. it would be best to have its own webpage 'i-Flyers', however the i-flyers could also be included on your 'News' or 'e/i-Newsletter' pages, etc.

Production of e-Flyers

A good e-flyer can be put together using the basic software - 'Office Word' or 'Office Publisher'. Otherwise, you may like to use more professional publishing programs, but these are usually not necessary, unless you have the expertise needed.

Save as .pdf files before uploading or emailing-out.

Often it is best to get a professional, usually your website's designer, to create **e/i-flyer and e/i-newsletter templates** based on your school website's templates. You then add the information and images (sometimes with graphics) as needed.

Database for email-outs

Create an email database of the interested parents and other individuals and groups.

i-Flyer Webpage

The simplest and easiest, yet least effective, method to publish an i-flyer is to place it only on your website.

If using this method, it would be a good idea to have a special webpage named 'i-flyer', or something similar which draws attention to its urgent / high priority nature. It should be placed on the specially created i-flyer template webpage.

The adding of content to this page would be of a similar nature to adding content to any of the other webpages on your website. Knowledge of these skills is necessary.

Layout

The heading / title would be devoted to the theme e.g. Swimming Carnival Thursday.

Follow this with key points and necessary detail. Remember the golden rule of marketing – **brevity, clarity and presentation**.

Place **attractive photos**, based on your theme, to gain greatest appeal. Captions are often essential.

Photos, brief text, color and branding (through the well developed template) are key aspects of any flyer.

Size

Often the best sized flyer is the equivalent of an A4 page.

You may also include links from the e-flyer / i-flyer to other webpages you would like linked, including your 'i-Newsletter', 'News' and 'Service Times' webpages.

Try not to allow these links to distract from your flyer's theme but to compliment it. Often the best position for links is at the bottom of the page. However, there would be times when linking directly from the text or image would be necessary or suitable.

A high quality production is necessary.

Production – Offsite Option

You may like to do everything onsite or send all resources to your third party e-flyer / i-flyer producer.

Production is similar to creating an advertisement:

- Sketch layout according to decided theme and placement on a e/i-flyer template
- Arrange images' placement. (Each image needs to be large enough to clearly see the required detail. Captions are often necessary to compliment the photo's message.)
- Write the text (e.g. Open Day text would need the details of the day including times, venue, displays, addresses, post event activities such as bbq, etc.)
- Select photos from any of last year's event, etc.
- Arrange for the taking of any other photos (photos) you need
- Make final photo selections (each photo tells a thousand words.)
- Discuss layout, texts and photos with the School Principal or designated personnel
- Include contact details for the school, especially addresses, website address, email address and phone number, at bottom of main page
- Proof all text and images
- Send sketches, images and texts for the e/i-flyer to the producers for layout arranging (unless completed at the School Office or through a parent's generosity – then send digital file by email or CD)
- Proof drafts received back, usually by email from producers, with the school Principal or other key personnel. Send back to producers for updating.
- Read final draft and when all changes have been made sign-off for publishing.
- Producers will now email this out to all on the database you have provided.

Sample e-Flyer

This is presented to parents and other interested people as one continuous page. Due to this e-books A4 size, the e-flyer has been segmented.

Having trouble viewing this email? <u>Click here</u> to view an online copy.

Send to a Friend | Update Your Subscription Details | Unsubscribe

17 February 2010

Dear Mr & Mrs Foster,

This week's tragic incident at St Patrick's College is a traumatic experience; certainly for those directly affected or for those who knew the victim. But trauma may be more wide-spread, as the sense of safety that we experience in school has been violated.

A traumatic event is a powerful and upsetting incident that may intrude into daily life. Some students and parents may be feeling unsafe and distressed that such an event could occur on an ordinary day in a school environment. However, it is important to remember that schools are safe places and that traumatic events such as this recent event are out of the ordinary and very rare in the Australian context. Currently, schools are well equipped to provide support to their communities as well as having access to specialist staff such as Guidance Counsellors to provide more in depth assistance as required.

Staff will be concerned about the emotional wellbeing of children in the schools, and many parents and caregivers will be looking for advice on how to respond to questions from students about an unsettling and upsetting traumatic event happening in a school situation. Many students will recognise that they have been through a distressing experience and it is important that they have permission to experience some reaction to it. Please contact a member of the Aquinas College Leadership Team or the Mr Wayne Mc Burnie College Counsellor Ph 55 102 888 if you require assistance in this area.

Please <u>click here </u>for further information.

Mrs Maryanne Finder
Principal

Aquinas College
Edmund Rice Drive,
Ashmore Qld 4214

Ph: (07) 5510 2888 | Fax: (07) 5510 2899

<u>Email Aquinas College</u> | <u>Visit the Aquinas College Website</u>

Please consider the environment, before printing this email!

This message (including attachments) is intended for the addressee named above. It may also be confidential, privileged and/or subject to copyright. If you are not the addressee named above, you must not disseminate, copy, communicate or otherwise use or take any action in reliance on this message. You understand that any privilege or confidentiality attached to this message is not waived, lost or destroyed because you have received this message in error. If you have received this message in error please notify the sender and delete from any computer. Unless explicitly attributed, the opinions expressed in this message do not necessarily represent the official position or opinions of Schoolzine Pty Ltd. Whilst all care has been taken, Schoolzine Pty Ltd disclaims all liability for loss or damage to person or property arising from this message being infected by computer virus or other contamination.

Social Networking Website Use for Schools

> Schools can benefit from appropriate, and sometimes creative, use of social networking sites.
>
> Increasingly, this form of communication is becoming more obvious for schools.
>
> Be aware of all the privacy and legal issues!

The Challenge

Once again we are challenged to meet our parents, staff, students and other interested community members where they are at, or might be, in the near future.

The **social networking tentacles are reaching further into the various demographics affecting our school communities,** often way beyond the awareness of school leaders.

No longer is it just the **teens and '20 something'**, it is **now common for people in their 50s and 60s** to have one or more social networking accounts.

Misconception?

With respect, and only to make a point shout out loudly, the misconception is that this form of communication is just used for inane chat amongst 'dizzy lightweights'!

Yes, this may be so for a number of users, however there is a considerably large and ever growing group of people who use this for much more than chat, even though legitimate chat does play an important part in many forms of communication.

These people are not only building and strengthening relationships amongst friends and newly formed acquaintances / friends through their engagement online with each other and often doing so simultaneously, they may also be **adding depth to key aspects of their lives**.

Underlying Assumptions

There are a number of interesting assumptions an ever expanding group of people, with representatives in most age groups, of the 21ˢᵗ century make:

- People like to build trusting relationships with others before doing 'business' (Schools need to be open to appreciating this belief and then adapting the way they communicate with such people.)
- The busyness of life often limits face-to-face opportunities
- The relationship does not need to be a face-to-face encounter, even though this is often preferred
- 'anonymity' allows for a less inhibited sharing of ideas and thoughts. (Easier for some people to make a comment when the contact person isn't actually in front of them. Similar for some people when using telephones or email.)
- The internet often provides the answers people are seeking (How often do you hear more and more, "Google it!")
- Digital communication is the easiest and quickest means of communication
- Digital communication allows for multiple conversations simultaneously
- People using these forms of communication eventually trust in the results due to their experiences.

Why Consider Social Networking Websites?

To reach this ever growing group of people in our communities we must meet them where they are at!

In many circumstances, this may not be your 'cup of tea'.
But you do have control over who sees and comments on your school 'Facebook' pages if you follow the security directions.

You may limit membership to only parents and former students (and students?) and hence only these people will see what you say and show.

Staff should not have students as 'friends' on their social networking pages due to the inappropriateness of this.

> It is, however, a successful method of informing an ever growing group of your community of whatever it is you would like to inform them about.

The examples below of the Aquinas College Facebook and Alumni Pages, shows some ways social networking sites e.g. Facebook is used by schools and past student associations:

- School and Contact Details
- News from the School Principal and Responses from Parents
- News about Students' Activities and Responses
- Upcoming School Events
- School Photos

Which Sites to Use

There are literally over 150 social networking sites available. An interesting article that explains the numerous options can be found at

http://en.wikipedia.org/wiki/List_of_social_networking_websites

It is generally agreed that the top three most popular sites, and hence the ones used by most parents, are 'Facebook', 'myspace' and 'Twitter'. 'LinkedIn' is at #5 and growing quickly.

This *School Marketing Manual for the Digital Age (2nd ed)* will concentrate on samples and instructions from: Facebook, Twitter and LinkedIn. Each website has its detail explained separately. Mention will be made of myspace.

Approaches to Use

There are two main approaches to using these social networking sites:

- As a school group
- As an school leader within the School

School Group Membership

Social networking sites have the capacity for you to form an educational group for your school.

I do not claim to be an expert in all the ways of any social networking site. I suggest that if you explore the social networking sites in greater depth, including various discussion boards, chat rooms, and blogs and use your search engines and the websites these find on the internet, you will gain a fuller appreciation of the positives and negatives of these sites.

For me these steps have been successful and up until this stage I have been more than happy with the results.

> I also believe that each educational system and institute needs to develop its own policies on this usage.

School Leader Membership

The school leader often gains considerable esteem from the parents and students who are social networking members or who may be considering being members.

The leader would often be the School Principal or other Leadership Team member. Of course anyone may have membership, **yet to speak on behalf of the school the person would need leadership approval.**

This page could be used for basic communication similar to a newsletter, or for whatever the School Principal or leadership team decides. It could be creatively used by these people to:

- Develop higher profiles
- Show another side to their personality, interests, etc.
- Explain their thoughts, beliefs and feelings on particular issues

Or to promote various happenings, such as:

- particular events or activities in which the school participates

Or to:

- Encourage involvement of others within the school community.

Caution - As with any use of the internet, privacy will always be an issue. The more information placed on the internet the more potential for this information being mis-used.

I would suggest that special care is taken with what is added to the internet.

I personally and professionally support the use of the internet. I believe that it has opened up so many positive options both personally and professionally.

I am always aware that I need to take due care with what I add to the internet.

If in doubt, always seek legal advice.

Check each social networking's privacy, safety and legal statements.

Facebook

Individual Sign Up Page

If you would like to set up an individual / personal Facebook page, go to the link below and follow the instructions similar to for the Group setup.

To create a **Facebook** account go to: http://www.facebook.com/

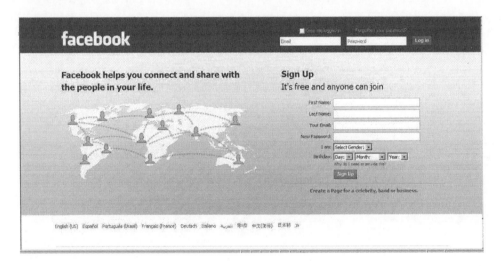

Sample Account

The following few screenshots are taken from my local Catholic Church Facebook and Parish Priest pages. This substitution for school and alumni Facebook pages was necessary so that I could avoid identifying various students, staff and other family members.

The approach used is the same for schools. Substitute School Principal or Leadership Team member for Parish Priest and School for the group.

A sample Facebook page extract by a Parish Priest is shown below with permission granted from Fr Adrian Sharp PP at http://www.facebook.com/adrian.sharp2?ref=ts

Religious Organization Sample

The following information and screen is included to help you with your development of a religious / educational group 'Facebook' page. These steps have worked for me on a number of occasions.

A parish which I have been heavily involved with for over a decade now has its own 'Facebook' group page. The St Mary's Catholic Community, Coomera 'Info' page is shown below with permission granted from Fr Adrian Sharp PP at:

http://www.facebook.com/group.php?gid=14891935948&ref=search&sid=1418024383.3181693141..1

The St Mary's Coomera 'Wall' page where members can add their own comments is shown below with permission granted from Fr Adrian Sharp PP at:

http://www.facebook.com/group.php?v=wall&ref=search&gid=14891935948

Messages are commonly added to the site e.g. the one below is found at: http://www.facebook.com/reqs.php

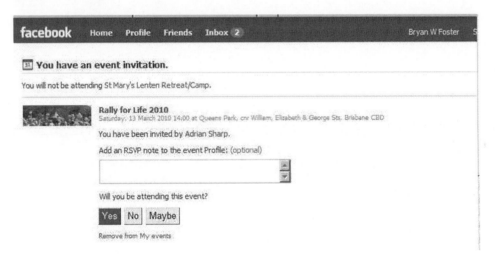

There are also various other religious organizations apart from churches and schools using Facebook. To find out what organizations have Facebook pages, just do a search when on a Facebook page. You will need to be a member of Facebook to do this.

Common groups for schools include the **school alumni** group.

Past students are some of the greatest supporters of the school and need to feel an integral part of the school. Their support is often through voluntary leadership and professional support, their children returning to the school, attendance at school events and financial support.

School Sign Up Steps Sample

As an example to show how to set up a Facebook group page, follow the webpages:

You begin on this Facebook homepage for membership @ http://www.facebook.com/

Next click on the bottom of this page where it says: "Create a Page for a celebrity, band or business. You then end up at the screen below.

Here select 'Area' then scroll down and select 'Education'. Or if you are a religious school you may like to initially select 'Brand, Product, or Organization' and then select 'Religious Organization'.

Next place the name of your Facebook page in the 'Name of Page' box. This would normally be the school and suburb. (The suburb helps differentiate from all the other schools in the world with your school's name.)

Tick the box just below so that this page won't go live on the internet just yet. I wanted to add to my profile.

(As I am not a school, for the purposes of this exercise I am calling the group - 'Love is the Meaning of Life'. This will help show the steps involved for group, i.e. school, membership.)

Complete the security check further down by placing the unclear letters from the box into the 'Text in the box' box.

Link School Account to Twitter?

When you go to the next page it will ask if you wish to link your new group page to your Twitter account. (See more about Twitter shortly.)

(For my newly formed group the next page appeared at: http://www.facebook.com/pages/Love-is-the-Meaning-of-Life/265813695571?created)

(Twitter Homepage may be found at: http://twitter.com/)

If you have a Twitter account this would probably be a good idea if you wanted to let your Twitter 'friends' see what you have added to your school Facebook site.

If you don't have a Twitter account (you can always make one later and come back to complete this request), or you do not want information you add to this site to go to Twitter, and then don't click on that option.

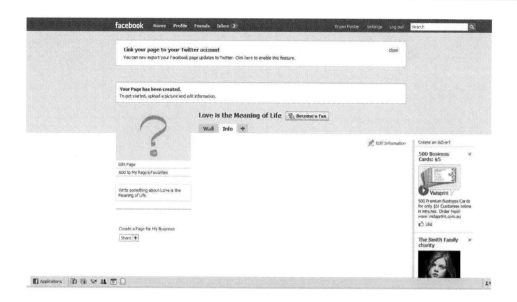

If you do click positively on this option you will end up looking at a similar page to this link:

https://twitter.com/oauth/authorize?oauth_token=w7vv0SUaJzN5xAseicYUCXphnvZ9xpf KJIA5ePeyrXo

I now have an account. At this stage I click on the name of my account i.e. 'Meaning of Life is Love' on the screen above (when it is live on my computer). The following screen comes up for me at: http://www.facebook.com/pages/Love-is-the-Meaning-of-Life/265813695571

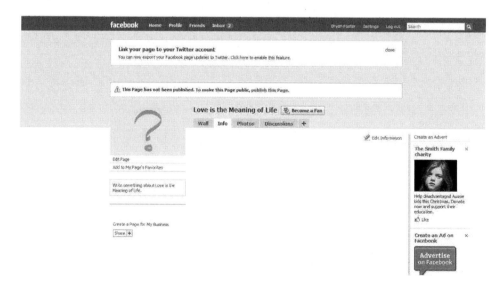

This is where we now add our initial detail about the School by clicking on 'Edit Information' on the right side.

We then add the various security levels, such as who can access the information, etc by clicking on 'Edit Page' in left column.

Then follow the prompts and complete as needed. There are many sections where you do not have to add anything if you do not want to… Just add what you are comfortable with.

Facebook FAQs and Help Webpages

A good selection of Frequently Asked Questions and Help for Facebook can be found at:

http://www.facebook.com/help/

Caution

I suggest that you read the following before commencing a 'Facebook' account to make sure this is best for you and your school.

Explore the Facebook Help webpage at http://www.facebook.com/help/ for Privacy, Security, Warnings, Intellectual Property, and Accessibility can be found at:

Twitter

Twitter is basically an abbreviated Blog.
It allows members instant messaging of thoughts of no more than 140 characters / spaces.
Tweets (responses) may also be added by mobile phone.

School Uses

- **Instant Feedback**

One key use of 'Twitter' could be to gain **instant appreciation of Parents and Senior Students' thoughts** on a topic.

For example - A data-projector could display the School's Twitter page on a large screen at an Information Night and Parents could instantly add their thoughts via their mobile phone to the account which would then be seen on the large screen instantly. This would give both instant feedback plus a record of views.

An example could be: a Parent offers a fund raising activity proposal and parents are invited to offer their first thoughts. Subsequent thoughts could be relayed later on. These are then taken to the leadership team for a decision and follow-up.

The school website may include a link to the School's Twitter account.

- **Interactive Classes**

The **modern teacher of senior students** could also include this as part of an **interactive lesson**. Imagine the **positive comment** this could bring to both the internal community and community at large!

Imagine offering the option for all students to comment on something being studied in class and their responses go up on the screen through the data projector. This could encourage the more introvert to offer an opinion. Their opinions should be of equal status to everyone else's – max 140 characters...

However, this could be open to problems, such as inappropriate 'live' comments. As with all other electronic / internet use in schools, this should be able to be dealt with accordingly. I do believe that in time these interactive classes will actually occur in various schools and suitable situations.

Various technical appreciation of how this works, protocols and parameters will be developed to suit individual schools and educational systems, etc.

- **Keeping in Contact**

This is another contemporary method for parents to keep in contact with key school personnel and vice versa.

It allows for **brevity of thought** – an often growing method of communication today. There are obvious downsides to brevity, on occasions, however if this form of communication gets various people to communicate, who would often not be so inclined, then surely this is a benefit.

All Twitter screenshots below are reproduced with permission of Twitter, Inc.

Twitter homepage may be found at http://twitter.com/

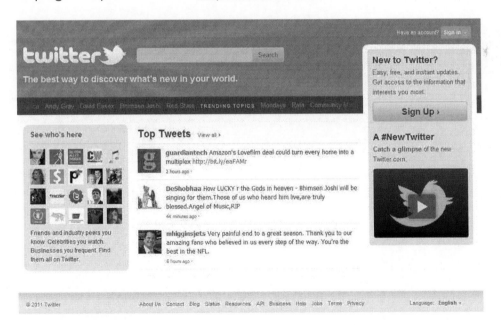

Twitter Explained Further

The Twitter About Us page has links to some good explanations about Twitter and may be found at http://twitter.com/about

Profile Page Example

As an example of a profile page, go to my personal profile page at http://twitter.com/aquinasrulz

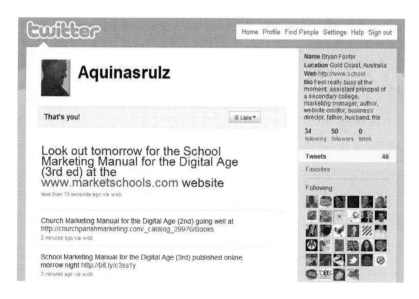

Home Page Sample

As an example of a Twitter homepage see my home page. This page is found at http://twitter.com/home

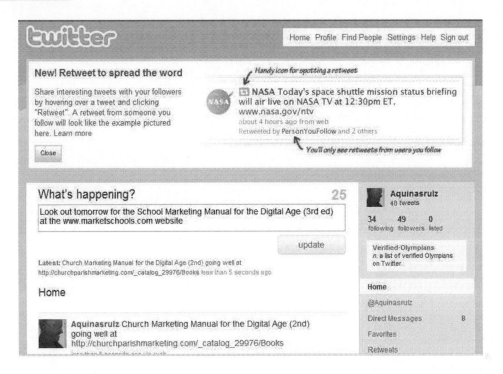

Privacy

I suggest you check out the Twitter Privacy statement before signing up. This statement is available at: http://twitter.com/privacy

Be aware that with all internet sites, especially social networking sites, your information may be seen by the general public. In certain circumstances viewing may be limited to selected people. Be fully aware of each website's Privacy and Terms and Conditions statements.

Sign Up

To commence a new Twitter account go to: https://twitter.com/signup

Twitter Groups

Be aware that Twitter Groups exist but at this stage are not a part of Twitter, Inc. itself. This may not suit your security or privacy concerns.

If you are interested in continuing to form a Twitter group go to http://twittgroups.com/confirm.php?oauth_token=d5G5hhEuJGJVY6cwtZjO9sMuqUtchAUfGtoLzTdltDs

This page details many of the group options available through this website.

You will need to then login to Twitter and continue the application process.

LinkedIn

> This is a social networking website for professional people.
> It opens up the opportunity to engage with another group of parents,
> potential families, business associates, past students, etc.

The same principles apply for use of this Social Networking Website as for the other previously explored.

Sign Up

To Sign Up go to: http://www.linkedin.com/

Sample Professional Page

A sample extract of my professional profile page is below and may be found at http://www.linkedin.com/myprofile?trk=hb_tab_pro

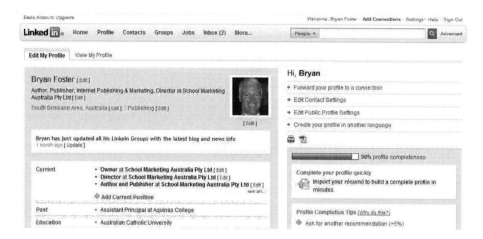

Form Groups for Discussion

There is also the option to form Groups for discussion purposes of topics relevant to the group. An example is my *School Marketing and School Marketing* Group seen at http://www.linkedin.com/groupAnswers?viewQuestions=&gid=2242227&forumID=3&sik=1265691816441&goback=%2Eand_2242227_13633837_1265691816439_*2

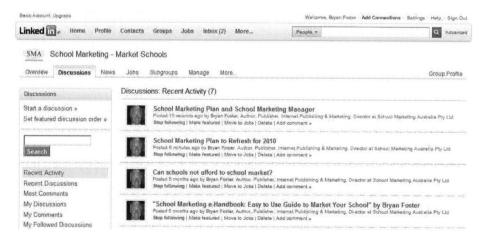

To create a group you will need to sign in and go to <u>http://www.linkedin.com/createGr</u> <u>oup?displayCreate=&trk=anet_creategrp</u>

Complete the form as requested and follow the prompts.

Privacy and Safety

Remember to read the <u>User Agreement</u> and <u>Privacy</u>.

Video Uploads

Including 'You Tube'

Uploading your school videos to your own school website
adds a special dimension for visitors to your site.
You may also consider uploading these to other video storage
sites for website flow increase + SEO advantages.

Uploading Video to School Website

I have found the easiest method for this, which has a double advantage, is to upload the video to 'You Tube' and then embed the video from You Tube into my website. This was initially as a recommendation from my web-builders.

This is a relatively simple procedure, plus it has the added bonus of increasing your website's SEO profile and traffic to your website through your school website links you have placed on You Tube when uploading your video to You Tube.

Let us start by uploading a video to You Tube.

Uploading Video to You Tube

Go to the You Tube homepage at http://www.youtube.com/ The appearance of this page varies continually as videos are uploaded. However, the basic template looks like the one below:

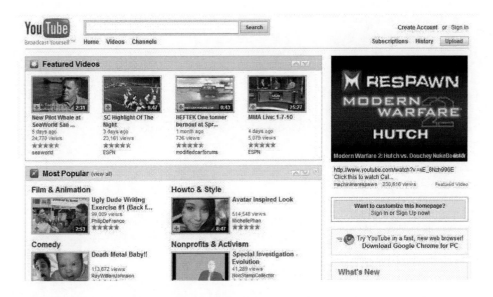

You will then need to click on the Create Account link in the top right hand corner and go to http://www.youtube.com/create_account:

Complete the online form to create an account.

Then click on Upload and follow directions to upload a video.

The following screen will appear from http://upload.youtube.com/my_videos

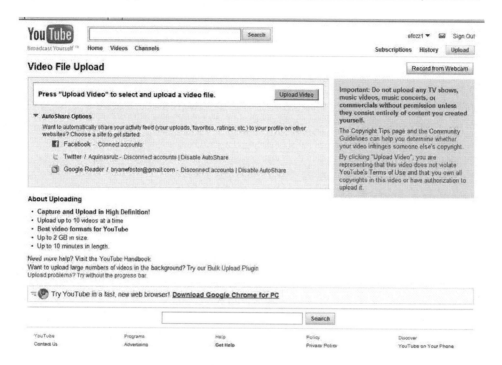

('Getting Started: Optimizing your video upload's on You Tube details the video specifications for best results at

http://www.google.com/support/youtube/bin/answer.py?answer=132460&tophoto=16612&hl=en-US

These webpages are not shown in this e-book. It also may be of interest that this webpage above also details information on HD formatted videos, how best to upload widescreen videos.)

Continuing with Uploading videos.

Next click on 'Upload Video' and you will go to the webpage below at http://upload.youtube.com/my_videos.

You will next need to select the video file from your computer. The uploading then begins.

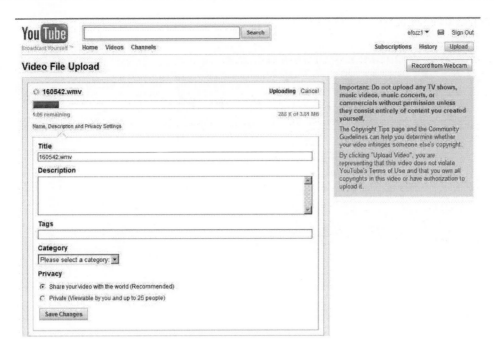

Next add a **Description,** in the Description box (see above image), of the video that is succinct and explains what the video is about and any purpose, etc needing to be stated.

Add **Tags** in the Tag box (see above image) similar as for Blogs i.e. a few key words and phrases that people might search for to discover your video in search engines. Select a Category and Privacy level.

Embed Video

In your You Tube account open the video you want to embed on the You Tube site. (See an example below, which is from my You Tube account.)

Click on the star at the end of the 'Embed' box in the right column.

Tick appropriate boxes as needed. Often I don't tick the 'Include related videos' box, as I would just like my video showing and not the option of others being selected by You Tube to also become available to the viewer of your video.

Select a color border if preferred, as well as the size it is to be on your screen, by clicking over your choices.

Normally select one of the first two sizes. Then highlight / select everything in the 'Embed box' as I have done in the sample below and Copy this.
This You Tube image comes from http://www.youtube.com/watch?v=nKnLepDczsM

Embed Video on Your Website

Go to the management software for your website, then to the webpage that you want to embed the video on. Next you will need to go to the HTML section for that page. In my software I click on the HTML button at the bottom of the webpage I want to embed the video onto. You will see it at the bottom left below.

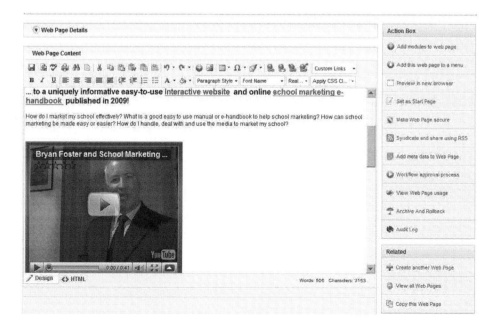

This takes me to the HTML script. I then find where I want the You Tube video embedded amongst all the text. In this particular case I look for the text with 'How do I handle, deal with and use the media to market my school?<' (see above the image on the screen) because these are the words immediately before where the embedding will occur.

See the highlighted text below. This is the actual text I copied off You Tube for embedding and then pasted to my management site in the appropriate position on the webpage that I wanted the video to appear.

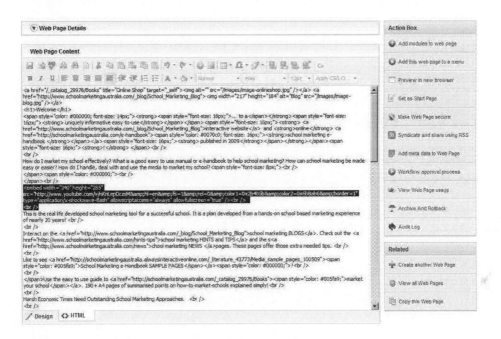

Save the page.

Check your website to see if the video is positioned as expected.

Repeat any of the processes as needed until all is correct.

You can also upload videos to other video storage websites apart from You Tube, such as *flickr* at http://www.flickr.com/ and *Daily Motion* at http://www.dailymotion.com/en.

The main reasons for this would be for:

- Search Engine Optimization or
- more traffic flow back through web-links to your school website.

Skype

> Skype allows for free calls across the internet between account holders.
> It allows callers with webcam to see each other.
> Another great school marketing opportunity!

Why Skype as part of the school marketing plan?

Apart from it being another technology that involves some or many of our school goers / Parents and that we need to meet these people where they are at, it is also:

- quite an exciting technological development
- one which should increase quite significantly in popularity over the short to midterm.

People are going to enjoy:

- cost benefits, which are free for the basic webcam usage
- time saving benefits -
- possibly be more willing on occasions to get into conversations from home / work with the School office personnel or other Parents, than actually meet with these people
- seeing the people who they interact with over the 'phone' (webcam) through their computer.

Skype Explained

Skype account holders may make FREE calls to each other between two internet connected computers and also to view each other via webcam i.e. video cameras built-in or attached / placed externally to the computers.

There are also **various options which require a payment**. Explore the Skype site for these.

Skype's main options are: Free calls between account holders, video calls and instant messaging over the internet. Plus phone calls to phones anywhere in the world for a fee.

This section will emphasize the free calls option whereby callers over the internet get to see each other as they speak.

For full details go to: www.skype.com

Specifically for video calling details go to:
http://www.skype.com/intl/en/allfeatures/videocall/

A reminder to also explore the Term and Polices at:
http://www.skype.com/intl/en/legal

To download Skype press the 'Download' button at:
http://www.skype.com/intl/en/download/skype/windows/

Below are the screens which will appear, at time of writing this text, as you progress through the Download. As part of the Download you will also be asked to '**Create a new Skype account**' as seen below.

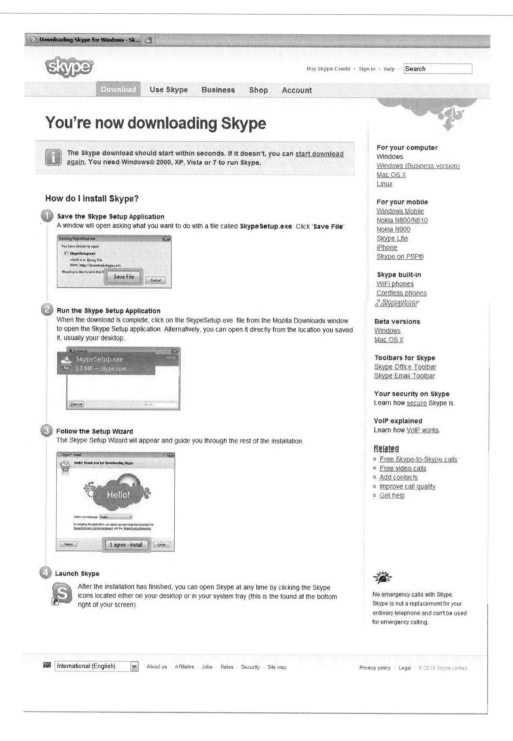

Continue following the prompts to achieve an account membership and the successful download of the software needed to operate Skype.

Enjoy this new and ever-expanding, inexpensive, very contemporary, communication option.

Build those school networks!

Chatting on the Web

by a Dad and his 15 year old

A most enjoyable experience was just had through discussing with my
15 year old the best use of chat rooms.
Chat rooms are good for use with younger people, particularly
for organizing something ...

Benefits of 'Chatting'

Below is an extract of the key points on the benefits of 'Chatting' ... in chat language...
ordered as per our conversation:

- to talk to people
- plan events
- keep in contact
- sometimes good because it doesn't need to be saved
- can be saved if you want
- mainly for chats between singles but you can talk to more than one person at a time, if you're organizing something, for example
- better than emails for group chats

The most appropriate use for chat rooms would be when conversing with or via young people to make arrangements for something e.g. a school social event, upcoming school celebration, etc,.

Chat Room for a School

A simple way to implement this school chat room for young people would be to engage a young/er person / teacher who the students of the school and the young of heart parents relate to and have him / her act as an intermediary with those charged with making the arrangements for the upcoming activity. This person would be a student leader or a young teacher, more than likely.

The leader would need to arrange for the young people to:

- all be 'friends' (members of their chat line group) on the chat line
- chat at a particular time and day
- develop an agenda, but not need to be too formalized, but be capable of 'going with the flow'
- make all 'friends' in the chat feel welcome and valued
- be able to lead a chat respectfully so as to achieve outcomes – emphasis is on 'chat' and not a 'meeting'
- call follow-up chats as needed
- feedback to key people within the organizational structure of the school
- feedback to other young people who weren't involved
- feedback to parents the process and outcomes – a well informed school is usually a supportive school.

Sample Chat Room and Sign Up Process

Hotmail at Windows Live is a popular chat room for young people. This chapter will use Hotmail as the sample study.

Another popular chat room is at Yahoo (see http://messenger.yahoo.com/ for details).

To begin the sign up process for Windows Live (including Hotmail) go to:

http://login.live.com/login.srf?wa=wsignin1.0&rpsnv=11&ct=1263351950&rver=6.0.5285.0&wp=MBI&wreply=http:%2F%2Fmail.live.com%2Fdefault.aspx&lc=1033&id=64855&mkt=en-au

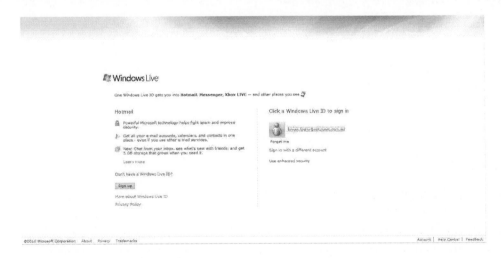

To find out more about the Hotmail click on 'Learn More' at the above site. This will take you to the screen below at http://mail.live.com/mail/about.aspx

You can either continue with the Sign Up by clicking on the 'Sign up' button on the first screen above at

http://login.live.com/login.srf?wa=wsignin1.0&rpsnv=11&ct=1263351950 &rver=6.0.5285.0&wp=MBI&wreply=http:%2F%2Fmail.live.com%2Fdefault. aspx&lc=1033&id=64855&mkt=en-au

or you may want to explore more about what Windows Live has to offer.

Overview of Windows Live Messenger

An overview of Windows Live Messenger (Hotmail is a part of this) may be found through the 'About' link at the very bottom of the page. This goes to http://download.live.com/

Here you will find much information about the options that Windows Live offers including:

- Messenger (Hotmail live chat – details follow in this text)
- Email
- Blogging – Writer
- Photos and Videos - editing and posting online – Photo Gallery and Movie Maker
- Web Browsing – Toolbar and Family Safety

All you do is go to this webpage and click on the links of interest. Attractive and informative pages appear. To find out more information, click on the links in the left hand column below the term 'Features'.

To download selected programs follow the instructions in the right hand column.

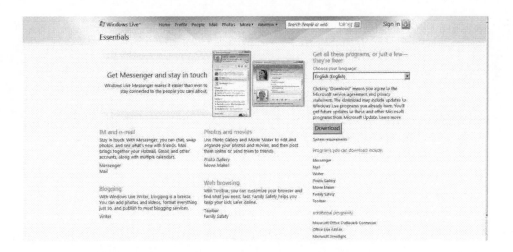

Click on 'Messenger' to get the general information webpage about the Chat option at http://download.live.com/messenger

This page has links to numerous areas of possible interest for you. You may like to explore these before proceeding.

Download Other Aspects of Windows Live

When ready Click on 'Download' and follow screen instructions.

Make sure you agree with the Microsoft service agreement and Privacy which are both found above the 'Download button' in the screen below or at the bottom of the following screen, the 'Create your Windows Live ID' screen.

Sign Up

To Sign Up and create your Windows Live ID for Hotmail go to the page below

https://signup.live.com/signup.aspx?ru=http%3a%2f%2fmail.live.com%2f%3frru%3dinbox&wa=wsignin1.0&rpsnv=11&ct=1263351950&rver=6.0.5285.0&wp=MBI&wreply=http:%2F%2Fmail.live.com%2Fdefault.aspx&lc=1033&id=64855&mkt=en-au&bk=1263351951&rollrs=12&lic=1

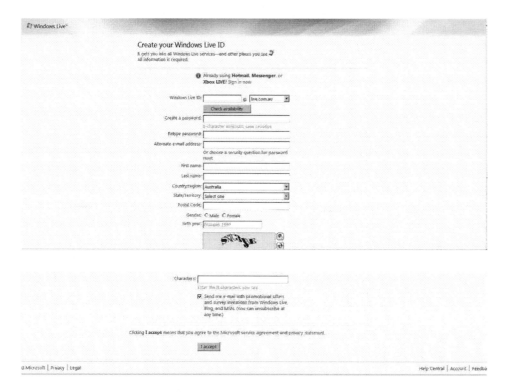

Once you click the 'I accept' button above you go to your Hotmail Inbox which is shown below. Mine is at http://mail.live.com/?rru=inbox

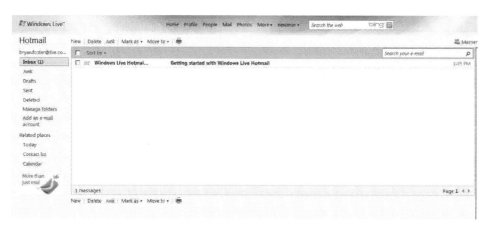

Click on 'Getting started with Windows Live Hotmail' in the Inbox above. For my account the link took me to my account at http://mail.live.com/?rru=inbox

To avoid confusion between Windows live and Hotmail see the following comment which is taken from the screen below:

"Hotmail is part of Windows Live.

Your Hotmail address and password give you free access to all Windows Live services so you can stay connected with the people and things that matter to you. Share photos, write a blog, get 25 GB of free online storage, and more."

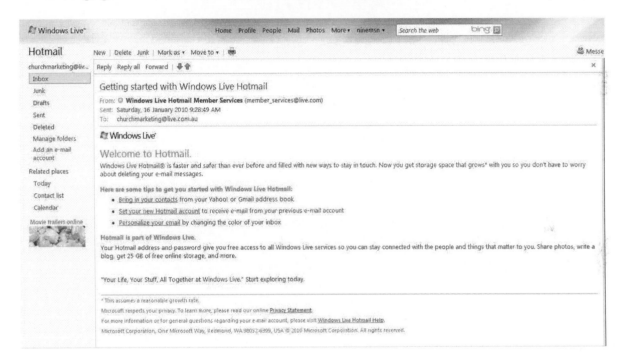

Another good Windows Live link is 'Get to Know Windows Live Hotmail' at http://www. windowslive-hotmail.com/LearnMore/

This webpage covers the topics:

- Personalize
- Protect
- Connect
- Organize
- Versatility
- Windows Live

Get Chatting

Once you have signed up, the Windows Live program will normally start when you open your computer. If it does not start automatically, then go to the toolbar on the bottom right of your screen. Click on the little person next to a green box (or wherever you have these toolbar placed) to open Windows Live. The screen which should appear is:

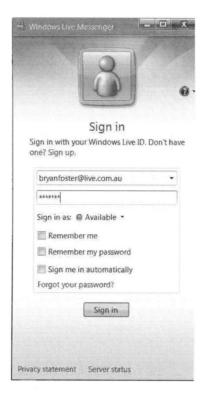

Next sign in your email address you used to sign up for this site plus your password and following the various prompts.

The first time you get connected a one-off screen will appear. It offers further assistance. Decide if you need to use its options or just close the window.

You will need to get 'friends' before you can begin chatting. Follow the instructions from this webpage.

Enjoy chatting, particularly in groups tasked with organizing events / activities!

School Marketing and the Traditional Media
+ Instructions

School Marketing and the Traditional Media + Instructions

Do not fear the media but be prepared!

All you are ever likely to need to know about dealing successfully with the media.

This e-chapter will help you deal with the journalists, photojournalists and media outlets to gain the best results for your school.

You are in charge but need to appreciate the role these people play in marketing your school.

The big challenges of writing media releases and editorials (stories) are clearly explained here. There is a sample to view!

Headings

- Media
- Media Releases
- Writing a Media Release (+ Sample)
- Media Interview
- Journalists Visit School
- Photojournalists at School
- Editorial from the School (+ Sample)
- The Difficult Media Situation
- Staged' events

Traditional Media

The traditional media - newspapers, magazines, radio, and television - still has a powerful influence on people's perceptions of schools.

Effectively using the media is of considerable advantage.
(It is also of benefit to the media.)

Do not be afraid of the media! Be respectful!

A common misconception is that the media will contact the school on a regular basis for stories. Most often this is not the case.

When a good relationship is developed between the school and the various media outlets, a balance and appreciation of each other's needs will be reached.

Positive Relations

Schools need to develop positive relations with the media.

Having the media work for you is a real advantage.

Also, having the media not work against you is another advantage.

Most media outlets want to work with schools to portray positive stories to their readers. These are the feel-good stories, which help sell newspapers, television and radio time.

This builds the media's advertising base, hence profits.

They are also seen as good community advocates.

> This positive relationship doesn't just happen.
>
> The School Marketing Manager, in particular, needs to develop
> this relationship in a number of ways.

These include contact with journalists, good media releases, advertising with them and the availability of the SMM to the media outlet.

School Contact Person

- **The SMM should be the known contact person for the media.**

To avoid confusion the media should be channeled through the SMM even though the issues may concern another staff member or student. School office personnel and other staff need to be aware of this.

The media would usually prefer to contact one person for ease.

- **Confusion may lead to unforeseen results.**

Confusion may exist when this doesn't occur. Sometimes the media get annoyed with perceived buck-passing.

Sometimes the School may get 'tricked', or not be fully aware of the line of enquiry, by a section of the media following up on a less than positive perceived or real story. This may occur when the media engages someone from the School who does not know how to deal with them or what should be released by the School on a particular issue.

The only exception should be a request to speak with the School Principal, as long as they are content with this procedure. Often the School Principal will seek the SMM's advice or that of the system's Communications and Marketing Manager before completing the media's request.

> The School Principal needs to make his role in certain media requests
> clear to the SMM to avoid any confusion.

Media Release

The SMM needs to provide stories to the media which they would want to run. This initially is given in the form of a media release. Follow-up telephone calls often assist the process.

The SMM should cultivate particular contacts within each media organization to facilitate the follow up of the media releases. (See 'Writing the Media Release')

Direct Contact with Media Outlets and Journalists

There are also certain types of stories for particular outlets. A sample of this would be the feature pages within a newspaper. These features often cover community activities in general and cover a wide variety of school / community themes e.g. sport, the arts, literature reviews, student written articles and other articles of interest to their readers.

These types of stories need a specific contact with that features subeditor, or journalist, and not a media release. A phone call from the SMM initially ascertains if there is particular interest in a suggestion. This is followed by further calls, emails, possible interviews and photo sessions, as needed, as the project develops.

> Having journalists who you can bounce ideas off to decide what is of interest, will invariably save time and gain a wider media acceptance of your ideas and the stories presented.

This further enhances your reputation with these journalists and the success rate for having stories covered.

Balanced Relationship is Needed

> A balance is needed in appreciating how much contact you should make via media releases and direct contact to journalists.
>
> Don't become the pest!

A problem develops when your media releases or phone calls become intrusive and overbearing. No-one wants to be harassed and journalists may feel this way if a balance on the amount of contact isn't reached.

> Sometimes it is a good idea to place yourself in their shoes.

How much contact for gaining stories would you like? Remember that you are not the only one with stories. Also, the subeditor has other expectations of the journalist and his / her need to meet these expectations.

SMM's Availability

The SMM should always give a response to a particular media request immediately.

However, you do not need to give the answers to their questions immediately.

Your response may be that you will get back to them shortly with their request. Make sure this happens within a reasonable time limit, say 30 minutes.

Often you will need to arrange for the principal, staff or students to be available for an interview and photo session. Or it may be for these people, to answer a few questions in an interview over the telephone.

Most stories the media wishes to cover can be arranged within a day or two. Sometimes this will need to be arranged in a couple of hours.

Be Careful – Do Not Seem Uninterested

If the media outlet feels as though you are not available or lack interest, they will go to another school or source for their request.

Each media outlet will have a short list of schools they will contact if they need a school's input or photo for a story. This list will change depending on the support given by those schools to the media's requests.

The Media Release

The media release is your way of informing the media of something special.

When Used

Mostly it is used to try to get coverage for a particular event or success about to occur, occurring, or recently occurred, within the school.

Sometimes it is used to advise the media of information necessary to allay any negative stories.

No Guarantees

There is no guarantee that the media will be interested in covering your story.

It is not easy getting the media to run your stories. There is much news out there and there are many schools vying for media space.

This may appear harsh, however if it was a 'big news' day your story may have been small in comparison. You may try again when a similar story occurs.

Experience will help you evaluate those stories which have more chance of successfully being picked up by various media outlets.

DO NOT GIVE UP!

Better Chances of Coverage

At least there will be times when there is that quiet news day when the media is looking for something within reason!

Keep your relationship with the media growing so that you will be considered, especially for these types of days.

The Christmas and summer holidays are a good time to get coverage. This is usually a quiet news time.

There will be times when you have a good success rate and other times when it seems that no matter what you offer no outlet is interested.

Long Dry Periods - Response

If the dry period is too long, you will need to develop other forms of media communication or expand on already used ones.

An example of this would be to write your own newsletter, and professionally produce this newsletter / booklet. A good size is A4 of about 12 to 16 pages in length.

(See more details on this form of 'do-it-yourself' publication in 'Commercially Produced Newsletter' section).

Another option would be for you to enhance your weekly e/i-newsletter or newsletter and / or increase its distribution list.

Don't forget the e/i-type of publication where you email out or have the publication placed on your webpage! (See e/i-Newsletter / Newsletter section in Resources portfolio.)

Advertising usually gains certain amounts of editorial space for certain sized adverts in various features in newspapers.

The feature sections are often pullout sections. Feature sections which often assist schools could be: Lifestyle, Community Service or Education.

The space allowed for editorial is usually in a 50/50 ratio if you use a certain sized larger advertisement. These advertisements are measured in column centimetres: so many columns wide by so many centimeters deep. Check with your outlets. (See 'Editorial from the School' section.)

'The Event' - Two Media Releases

> Two media releases are often found to be the best approach for each event that is about to occur and which you would like to have covered.

The first is sent a day or two before for a normal event. However, you may need to send it a week before for a major big story event e.g. 50th anniversary of the school or new facility opening.

> The first media release gives details necessary to gain interest

This hopefully gains a telephone request from the media for more details or for an interview and / or photo request.

The second media release should be sent very early on the day of the event - best before 8am.

This gives more detail and acts as an enticement.

> The second media release also repeats in a different way the main points from the first media release and adds necessary new information.

The second media release needs to emphasise the logistics of when, where and who is involved.

> You may also need to follow-up the 'big event' media release with a call to your contacts in the various outlets or to the outlets in general requesting to speak with a journalist re a recently sent media release regarding a major event.

Media Webpages – Align Stories for...

Most media outlets use their websites for key promotion of their main stories, plus as an archive. These archives can store stories for quite a considerable time.

The website presentation is quite spectacular with all its color and clever web-design. Your story usually looks very good in these conditions. Promote its presence through your school website, newsletters, flyers, etc.

Keeping this in mind, write media releases and send colorful creative photos to enhance the story.

An example of a recent story from my school headed 'College reaches out' may be found at:http://www.catholicleader.com.au/news.php/schools-news/college-reaches-out_54521

Reproduced with permission from The Catholic Leader and Aquinas College, Southport.

Writing the Media Release + Sample

Media Release Writing Skills

> Develop effective Media Release writing skills so as to gain media coverage.
>
> This is often your best means of gaining this somewhat difficult exposure.

The media release should ideally be kept to one page to be effective. (See Sample at end of this chapter.)

> One of the major difficulties found when beginning to write media releases is keeping the length relatively short.
> There is often a desire to give all the detail because you believe it enhances your case.

Sometimes a little more detail is needed, but not to the detriment of the success of the media release.

You may also attach supporting documentation. Supporting documentation is usually better than an extended release. It breaks up a long media release.

A media release is often read if the heading and introduction is captivating.

Long releases can be considered boring and hence not read.

> Remember that the media outlets are receiving an enormous number of releases daily. The best media releases and best stories usually gain the best attention.

Sending a Media Release

- The media release is printed onto the school's letterhead paper before transmission.
- The media release is next faxed (or emailed, usually with prior arrangements) to the chosen media outlets.
- In most cases this is to a list of media outlets which should have been stored prior in the memory of the fax machine's / email group list.
- Emailing is currently gaining more of a general acceptance from the media for media releases. You need to know each outlet's expectations.
- If they are not email interested, you may still be able to arrange emails with specific contacts for certain focused stories e.g. school feature pages within the local newspaper.
- Follow-up phone calls may need to be made if there is no response or if you just want to keep building on your relationship. Remember not to overdo this though.

Response of Media to an Event

- Media representatives will usually contact you if there is an interest.
- The media may not always respond to your media release but may just turn up a few minutes before the event ready to do the coverage.
- Have someone prepared to meet them in the School Office if you know they will be there or have some other contingency plans just in case they arrive without you knowing.
- Be courteous and welcoming, have them sign in and then taken to the venue. They should then be introduced to the SMM who then helps them out.

Suggested Media Release Outline Plan:

- On School letterhead stationery
- Banner stating: <u>MEDIA RELEASE</u> (in very large, bold letters e.g. 72 point size)
- Date below stating: <u>For immediate release: List Date</u> (in large letters e.g. 22 point size).
  (You always have the right to place an embargo on the release to a later specified date. However, from a school's point of view, this would hardly, if ever, occur. If an embargo is placed on the release date of the story write this embargoed date: <u>Embargoed release: List Date</u>)
- Heading in large, bold letters (about 22 point size). Keep it as brief as possible. The heading should immediately capture the reader's attention, such that they wish to read on.
- Bulk of release: Needs to be in order of priority of points. Main points at the beginning and lesser points at end, in normal 12 point font size.
- The lead paragraph is critical to gaining attention. It should be your main point.

> - The reader at the media outlet will only read what they find interesting. If you leave important points to the end of the media release these might not get read because the reader may have stopped reading and already disposed of your media release.

- The release should be written in succinct short paragraphs, often in single sentences for effect.
- Quotes from key people should most often be included. These would usually come from the School Principal and other key people noted in the release. Best to have no more than two people quoted, but preferably only one. This saves on confusion and the release becoming too wordy.
- If more than one page use: .../PTO
- End with: .../end
- If the request is for the media's presence at an event, etc, repeat or highlight at the end of the media release in a separate succinct sentence in bold type the key details which tell the journalist where and when they need to be at a particular venue.
- Below this add the details of who authorized the media release and contact details including mobile / cell number and email address. Without this the release has no real authority and no-one to contact. Remember, you are hoping for a visit on the day of the event or contact for success.

Sample follows...

(NB - On School Letterhead Document)

MEDIA RELEASE

For immediate release: 3 April, 2010

Huge Easter Liturgy throughout the College campus tomorrow at 10am

Easter will be celebrated at Aquinas College tomorrow with the dramatic annual Easter Liturgy. The liturgy depicts significant moments in the last days of the life of Jesus.

Palm Sunday begins in the Middle School Area, the Last Supper, Trial and 39 Lashes in the Assembly Area, the Crucifixion at the Drama Centre and the Resurrection in Mary Immaculate Church.

Over 60 students are directly involved as actors, dancers, musicians and singers. The remainder of the College jeers during the trial and places colorful flowers on the cross at the resurrection. A spectacular freeze of Jesus in the arms of Mary at the foot of the cross under red lights occurs in the Drama Centre after the crucifixion.

"This spectacular liturgy is a wonderful way for the Aquinas' community to celebrate Easter. The students' involvement is something to see," said Mrs. Maryanne Finder, Principal.

The liturgy begins in the College Assembly Area at 10am and concludes in the Mary Immaculate Church around 11:30am

Many unique photo opportunities exist.

Authorized by: Bryan Foster, Assistant Principal / School Marketing Manager
[Telephone and email contact detail]

The Media Interview

Be well prepared!

> The media interview is a very important means of getting your message across to an outside media outlet.
>
> Again - Be well prepared!

The interview is usually conducted by a journalist at the school.

Sometimes over-the-phone interviews occur.

Who is interviewed?

Students are mostly interviewed. Sometimes the Principal and various staff members may be interviewed.

Often the SMM will be interviewed but this is mainly as a result of clarification being needed by the journalist for a particular story or upcoming interview. The SMM may be asked to give quick quotes for the completion of a story or for an addition to a news story requiring a school's input.

The SMM may need to seek the Principal's input for these types of quotes.

The SMM may need to obtain a quote from the Principal.

Preparation for the interview

School representatives need to be well prepared for any interview.

> If possible, practice interviews should be conducted before the journalist arrives.

> The SMM should pre-empt possible questions for those being interviewed.

Even if the interviewee is the only person who knows the detail being sort, the SMM's preparedness is required.

Go over with the interviewee what the procedure will be and possible questions.

The SMM needs to build confidence in the person about to be interviewed.

This is best done through thorough preparation. People feel more confident when questioned on areas for which they are prepared.

> Concentrating on the key 3-4 points you want to get across is often the best and easiest way of approaching the preparation and interview.

> However, it is also necessary to try and pre-empt possible 'curly' questions and develop possible responses.

Prior to the journalist arriving, the SMM should make firm plans with those to be interviewed to meet at a designated time and at a designated place. This allows the SMM to ascertain whether everyone is present and if any last minute change of arrangements is required.

Sometimes the journalist is late.

This is unfortunate; however it is best to make plans to suit the journalists for as soon as they are able to arrive. This sometimes causes great inconvenience to the school, interviewees and SMM.

Sometimes either the journalist or photojournalist arrives at different times. This isn't usually a problem as it is possible to start with just one present.

Conducting the Interview:

- The SMM would meet the journalist and often a photojournalist at the School Office. Welcome them appropriately and have them sign in. They may need to wear school endorsed name tags while in the school grounds.
- Offer them a non-alcoholic drink.
- Have a predetermined venue on offer, whether indoors or outdoors depending on the nature of the story and weather conditions at that moment. Offer this suggestion to the journalist who will usually accept.
- Have a chat about where you are about to go, the interviewees involved and any restrictions e.g. time restrictions that may be apparent.
- The SMM then takes the journalists and interviewees to the selected venue/s.
- If some photos are being taken at the same time as some interviews, the SMM will need to arrange for another well informed staff member to assist the photojournalist.
- The SMM, or any designated staff member, should usually remain with the journalists until they leave the school grounds.

SMM at Interview

- The SMM must maintain control over the interview situation but in a quiet, non-threatening way.
- The SMM, or a well informed staff member designate, needs to be present at all interviews with students. The main reason is as a duty of care. It is beneficial to be present at staff interviews also.
- The SMM's presence helps the student or staff member be more at ease through having a supportive staff member at the interview.
- The SMM may also be called upon by either party for assistance or clarification.

- The interviewee needs to appreciate that the interview is to be conducted for a positive outcome.

- Only positive points should be discussed.

Negative Questions – A Response Method

Anticipate the sort of negative questions which might arise and prepare good responses.

Have your key 3-4 positive points you would like to make.

Key techniques during the interview are:

1. Acknowledge the weakness (apologize if needed)

2. Agree that plans are afoot to improve the situation

3. Continually revert back to the 3 key positive points you want to make

It may also be necessary to make arrangements with the interviewee prior to the interview, and before the journalist arrives, that the SMM would interject respectfully if the interviewee was getting particularly stressed or confused during the interview.

An example could be if the interviewer says that it must get very boring climbing up diving towers and jumping off for a few hours a day, then remind the student that it could appear boring but that the benefits of all this hard work far outweigh the hard effort given in training.

It is often best to do this in a light-hearted manner and preferably in a fun way.

Journalists Visiting the School

As a general rule, the SMM or designate should always be with the journalists while they are in the school grounds.

Meeting Time

The SMM needs to be accurate with the time given for the journalists to be present e.g. advise that the function starts at 6pm, the guest speaker will speak at 6:10pm and the speaker will be available for interview at 7pm.

Journalists' schedules are often tight, which means they have a specific time to leave for their next appointment.

The interview time arranged needs to be met.

They should be welcomed, signed-in if necessary and offered a non-alcoholic drink. They will often not accept these unless they are early or the event / interview is late and they have some leeway time.

Coverage of an Event and SMM's Role

Until a good rapport with various journalists is developed, it is best for the SMM or designate to be with them while they are in the school's grounds covering specific events.

The SMM or designate should always be present with the journalist or photojournalist at interviews and photo taking.

The designate would need a thorough briefing beforehand on their role, what they should do and possibly some of the things that they should say.

> It is suggested that you do not take anything for granted in assuming
> this designated person knows what to do.
>
> You need to fully inform him / her.

Once a rapport is developed over time, the journalists are most likely capable of being trusted to move around appropriately to listen, video or take photos of these events e.g. School Assembly where a special guest from a local service group is receiving the school's large donation of goods and cash.

If an interview or a posed photo is required after the event, the SMM or designate needs to be present.

This allows him / her to maintain control, help with setting up for photos or interviews and assist those about to be interviewed.

> The SMM is also a supportive presence and
> someone who can usually allay the nerves of those involved.

> The SMM should not let the journalists do anything s/he is not happy about.
> You have a right to step in if necessary.
>
> You are responsible for the students in your care and hence those being interviewed or photographed may need your assistance.

Be reasonable though, remembering that the journalists are doing their job and in most cases are on your side.

> Know your legal and ethical responsibilities.
>
> Seek these from qualified legal practitioners and ethicists.

Photojournalists

Overview

> Photojournalists are responsible for getting the best photos they can for their particular media outlets.

Photojournalists will most likely have good ideas to best represent the image you want covered.

> The SMM, or selected well informed staff member, needs to attend all photo sessions.

Photo sessions are usually enjoyable times for all involved. It is not often that people appear in the media. The SMM should treat it as an enjoyable time and it most likely will end up being so.

The photojournalist usually works with the journalist who is covering the story. Yet it is often the photojournalist who decides which photos will be used.

There will be times when the media outlet only wants a photo and just sends a photojournalist.

At other times you will need to arrange for interviews and photos at the same or similar times.

However, at other times, the interview may happen over the telephone and the photo taken at a separate time.

Even though most stories require a photo, sometimes it is not required.

Own School Photos

There may also be times when the media outlet is quite happy for you to send your own photos by email instead of having the photojournalist come out.

This usually happens after the outlet appreciates the quality and content of your school's photos and the professionalism of your photographers.

This is more common with the smaller publications, or for photos accompanying editorial in special features and for advertising.

Rest assured that the outlets will invariably send out a photographer if you feel you need one.

SMM and the Photojournalist

You are free to offer suggestions, though the final decision does rest with the photojournalist.

Their employer is their media outlet (and not your school) and hence the photo taken is what they want.

However, in most cases, the photojournalist is working with you and for the school to be seen in the best light.

It is in their best interests to work with you for many reasons, including the media outlet's need for a good standing in the educational and wider community. They will also possibly want photos, reactions or stories from your school down the track.

However, if you are being unfairly obstructive, then follow-up photos for other stories at other times may be few and far between.

Stopping Inappropriate Photos and Follow-Up

You must make sure that the photos taken are appropriate for student, staff member and school.

Do not allow for anything raunchy or what might appear inappropriate.

It is strongly suggested that students and staff in the photo shouldn't:

- hold any inappropriate prop e.g. cigarette
- appear before an inappropriate backdrop e.g. toilet or certain signage
- wear inappropriate clothing e.g. skimpy tops or skirts
- be positioned in any inappropriate manner e.g. sitting inappropriately.

> If you are not happy with the photojournalist's suggestions, then stop the photo shoot, negotiate a better outcome, or cancel it.
>
> You are responsible for trying to get the best most appropriate photo.

You have every right to do this - in fact you may have a responsibility to do this.

Advise your School Principal of this situation and outcome.

> Know your legal and ethical responsibilities.
>
> Seek these from qualified legal practitioners and ethicists.

If the photo session was cancelled, you or your School Principal would seriously consider contacting the media outlet's editor and advising of the inappropriateness of the photo-journalist's expectations / demands. This should sort the problem out.

Further courses of action, if no success in the first instance was gained from the editor, would often be to contact your educational system's Communication and Marketing Manager for guidance and support.

Either your School Principal or the Communication and Marketing Manager would probably take the matter further e.g. journalists' association, members of parliament, etc, and even to police / court if there was any abuse. This would be a very rare indeed.

Editorial from the School + Sample

When Needed

Throughout the year you will be required to write editorial for various media outlets.

This is more than likely the result of the provision of free editorial with certain sized advertisements in special newspaper or magazine features.

Due to the number of schools and other community organizations trying to gain media attention, for most schools free editorial accompanying paid feature advertisements would be the only way of having editorial published.

Rarely, it may be the result of an invitation from the media outlet e.g. 50th anniversary of the school or for Education Week. Usually these events would be covered by media releases or as a part of a paid advertising package.

What is editorial?

Editorial is the 'story' component in the media outlet's production.

At times you may be asked to provide editorial i.e. a story to usually accompany an advertisement of a certain size, along with photo/s. (See Sample Below.)

The editorial is similar to a media release on the selected theme/s but with more of an advertising component. The media outlets normally allow for these to be virtually advertorials i.e. an advertising editorial. You would be promoting your school.

It is written in the same format as a media release (see 'Writing a Media Release').

It is often longer than a media release, therefore has more content and detail.

The space available will often match the space the advertisement takes.

You will also need to allow for a photo. Editorial is boring without a photo.

Remember that a photo 'tells thousands of words'.

The photo is normally selected from one or more that you send to the outlet.

Most outlets will send a photographer or photojournalist if you would rather this.

Advertisements Without Editorial

Placing advertisements outside special feature sections of publications i.e. in the body of the paper, or below the required size for gaining editorials as part of a feature's section, will generally not have the option of including editorials.

Way to Gain Editorial?

If you are a good advertising client or the paper needs to fill space, you may gain the occasional free editorial. This is very rare though.

Steps for Creating Editorial:

- The media outlet would contact you once you have confirmed the booking of an appropriate sized advertisement as part of a feature section.
- The contacting journalist will be either from the media outlet or from a journalist consultancy company. The outside consultants do the work of a normal journalist and then send the finished product to that outlet.
- You will be usually asked to provide details for them to create a story for you. You will also be asked for a time for them to send a photographer / photojournalist to the school. They are prepared to do as much as possible for you.
- The details you send are best sent in the format of a media release. This allows the journalist to see your priorities and the emphasis you would like to make.

When you gain experience in media release writing for editorial, you will often find that the journalist will select much of your release verbatim.

This is a real credit to you and an advantage to the school because the message you wanted published for the community has been achieved.

- The number of words required varies and you will normally be advised of this. If not, you should ask for the number. You need to keep fairly close to this word count.
- However, if you go beyond the requested number of words and your content is very good, and space is available, you may gain a longer published story. Best not count on this as it is the exception and not the rule.

Photos

> With experience you will know the types of photos that best suit certain stories and which would be acceptable to the outlet.

If there is a photo that you really want published, and it is of the quality required of the media outlet, then just send it. They will advise if it doesn't suit and discuss other options with you.

> If unsure, it is best to send a small selection, say 3-4 photos, which you would be happy to have published, and allow the journalist to decide.

Offer captions to explain each photo. (See sample below on school stationery.)

New DVD tells all about X College

Staff and students of [Name] College produced a new DVD which gives a dynamic and honest view of the College.

Mrs. Maryanne Finder, Principal, began the DVD emphasizing the welcoming and respectful nature of the College and its quality education.

"[Name] College offers a quality, Catholic education for all our students. As stated in our Vision and Mission statement, we value a welcoming community where students are safe, happy, can learn and are treated with respect," said Mrs. Finder, Principal.

[Student name] from Year 8 also emphasized the friendly nature of the College when she stated her personal thoughts on the DVD.

"[Name College] is a friendly community and I feel very welcome," said [Student name], Year 8 student.

Video images of the College are used throughout the DVD to show many outstanding aspects of life at [Name College].

High values are emphasized by Mrs. Maryanne Finder as the cornerstone of this very successful College.

"Our relationships are built on integrity and compassion, justice and mercy, forgiveness and love."

Mrs. Finder spoke of valuing the dynamic, challenging, rich and diverse curriculum and learning experiences.

[Name] Captains, [names], also emphasized the diverse curriculum and extra curricula opportunities, especially academic subjects and vocational subjects, the Sporting Program, Musicals, Rock and Dance Eisteddfods, Pastoral Care, IT, camps and retreats.

The new DVD is part of the enrolment package and may be obtained by ringing the College on [number] or emailing the College Secretary at: info@abc.qld.edu.au.

Pics 022 and 026: College Captains [Names] during videoing of the new [Name] College DVD. (Preference is for one of these two.)

Pic 027: Year 8 student [Student name] during videoing of the new [Name] College DVD

Authorized by: Name, Role, [Name] College phone / fax / mobile or cell, email address.

The Difficult Media Situation

Sometimes the media request an interview with no forewarning.

This usually happens when a story is considered 'big' and difficult.

Overview

This may be when something controversial or of a significant status has occurred and the media wants to run with that story on that day or the next.

Examples of these would include:

- a disaster where the school has had major damage, such as from a major storm or fire
- a staff member or school employee has been allegedly involved with something illegal
- a former staff member or school student has done something highly successful, controversial or allegedly illegal
- the government or local council have or will make a decision that impacts significantly on the, etc.

School Response

In this case initially you need to advise the media that the school representative, through the School Principal, yourself or someone else, will speak with them shortly [advise when e.g. between 30-60 minutes]. Best not to be more than 30-60 minutes, so that your response will be heard and not ignored!

You have every right to consider your options before speaking.

It is often best to contact the diocesan Communications and Marketing Manager, if such a role exists. This manager is usually familiar with best practice for such events. The manager will either become directly involved and speak on behalf of the school or offer suggestions on the best approach. The manager may also contact others within or outside the educational system who may be able to offer advice e.g. lawyers, building or insurance advisors / consultants, counselors, etc.

Offering a "No comment" is often fraught with potential misinterpretation or even worse. The outlet could, in this situation, just take the story according to the information they have, which may not be the truth or whole truth.

Comment truthfully.

You do not need to give all the details but offer what is needed for the media enquiry allowing for privacy and ethical considerations.

This may be just a simple, "Thank you for the enquiry. We will get back to you shortly."

If the school decides to act on the request itself there are a number of approaches which should benefit the school:

- Be available for an interview in person or over the phone
- Be positive and in control during the interview
- Appearance is important e.g. appropriate demeanour, dress, stance
- Control the backdrop for television or newspaper photo to get the positive visual message out that you want
- Answer all questions, but turn the answer to what you want to emphasize
- Having 3 key points to direct to the media is a good approach
- State the obvious, such as:
    * no one was hurt / unfortunately some people were injured
    * damage to the property was significant / minimal
    * the most important thing is that no-one was hurt, only property damage occurred and that this will be repaired as soon as possible or
    * unfortunately some people were hurt and the school is currently doing everything possible for those people e.g. ambulance was called immediately, there will be ongoing medical assistance, a counselor is involved for those directly affected, other counselors are coming from sister schools, etc.
    * the School Principal is sorry that this unfortunate event occurred, all procedures have been followed and that everything possible will be done
    * to ensure that this won't happen again.

    * If updating procedures is necessary then this will be done immediately.

Criminal Matters

For potential criminal matters refer the media to a specific contact at the educational system level (who you have forewarned and briefed in detail) who would be best placed to deal with that situation.

Follow-up

Be available to keep the media updated as the situation changes or developments are made.

Keep well advised, especially from the educational systemic level.

For criminal matters follow the educational system's advice throughout the whole process.

Staff Preparation for Interviews

- Personnel who will appear on television, radio or within print should practise the skills needed to be successful. It can be quite daunting when someone with a camera or microphone requests you to speak.
- You need to appear to be coherent, informed and in control. It is even more confronting when there are a number of cameras, microphones and people standing before you, particularly if it is due to a serious nature.

> Practise, practise, practise your interview techniques.

> Use video cameras and audio recording devices to record your responses and then learn from your experiences.

> Have selected staff members act as journalists and have them interview you.
>
> Allow for the difficult questions because this is part of the process.

> Remember, to keep coming back to your 3 key positive points.
>
> Be as positive as possible.

'Staged' Events

A number of events may be 'staged' for optimum media / marketing coverage throughout the year.

Defined

These events would most often be special / different / controversial / outstanding school events which would be heavily marketed, with a primary marketing aim of gaining some media coverage.

The secondary aim is usually something special for the school.

The desired media involvement would be free coverage gained as a result of media releases and / or phone calls to key media people.

Main Events

The main events for most schools are:

- Open Day
- Night of Excellence / Awards Night
- special celebrations done very well or differently e.g. Holy Week, Christmas and School Feast Day
- sports grand final game e.g. Firsts
- school musical
- past students' event
- school's feast day
- graduation day
- school formal
- major social / social justice / prayerful occasions
- arrival of a new Principal
- special donations / community involvement

Two events, which have been found to be very successful at Aquinas College, were a special Phone-a-thon and a unique Liturgy.

The Phone-a-thon was set up with the local television station and went live to air during and after the local news and weather segments. The purpose was to track down past students from the College for an upcoming major school anniversary. The setting was a room with a number of key people, including the Principal, a past Principal, staff member, student and SMM - all with telephones. On-air the SMM asked people to ring in details and also had a little 'chat' about the event with the host. The whole promotion went very well and was free of charge.

The Easter Liturgy is still covered yearly by the local television station and major newspaper. Its significance is its size, number of students in costume or otherwise involved, scenes and props used throughout the school campus and local church, and vision of whole school being involved with each new station of the cross. The Principal, students or SMM are interviewed by various media outlets each year.

Something Different

You might like to try:

- Being brave and prepared to hear from the general public suggestions to improve your school - being open to receiving all sorts of positive but also confronting 'suggestions'
- taking a social justice stance on a key issue and going to the public for support - encouraging attendance at information sessions given by special guests / personalities, letter writing, protests, prayer vigils, etc.
- tracking down past students for a 50th / 75th / 100th anniversary, etc.

Other Possible Events

- School Recognition Night (awards for special endeavors throughout the year...)
- Sports Night
- Bishop's visit, linked to something unique within the school / community
- School Dinner and special after dinner speaker

The event, or aspects / moments within it, should be as unique as possible to gain media attention.

The staged event then becomes the focus of a marketing campaign.

School Marketing Advertising in the Traditional Media

School Marketing Advertising in the Traditional Media

Advertising in the media is the most common form of commercial advertising used by schools. When done properly it is a very effective form of advertising.

This chapter will introduce you to these various forms of advertising and most importantly in simple to read summarized points show how to go about creating advertisements for each form.

Being well prepared with background material and prepared to oversee production and / or final advert presentation is necessary for success. This portfolio will explain how to do all this in simple easy to read ways.

Headings

Advertising in the Media
Newspaper and Magazine Advertising
Creating a Newspaper or Magazine Advertisement
Radio Advertising
Creating a Radio Advertisement (+ Sample)
Television Advertising
Creating a Television Advertisement

Advertising in the Traditional Media

This form of advertising is for a broad reach within society.

It goes well beyond the school community.

Common forms include: newspaper, radio, television and magazines.

Purpose and Overview

This form of advertising is mainly used to:

- Reach a broad audience beyond the school community
- Build a reputation within the broader community
- Have the reputation created support those within the school community
- Advise the broader community of the advantages of your school to society
- Encourage parents and their child/ren to consider enrolling in your school.

Success rates will vary depending on each individual publication and geographical location.

Advertising costs will also vary according to each individual publication and location.

Thorough cost analysis needs to be done by the SMM prior to developing a School Marketing Plan (SMP).

Often the smaller more localized publications are the best value as they often cost less and usually reach the targeted audience more effectively.

However, you need to be satisfied about:

- outlet's philosophy
- usual content
- style of presentation

- advertisement placement positions
- distribution method.

Advertisement Creation Options

- **Two options are usually available:**

    * The school creates and produces its own advertisement or
    * The media outlet creates it for you

Each media outlet would normally create the advertisement for you, if you so wish. You should provide as much information and as many resources as possible, particularly the branding style needed (see 'Branding').

Don't expect this method to be thoroughly to your liking though. You may need to go back and forth with the outlet until satisfied.

- **Background preparation**

> A database of resources is best to be created prior to the SMP's advertising campaign each year.

This database would include, where possible:

- Themes
- Layout designs
- Photographs
- Advert wordings
- School contact details

> Uniformity, according to the decided branding style, is essential for each advertisement.

> For a new SMM - in the early stages it might take some time to develop the database as you discover what works successfully.

- **Be prepared**

It is best not to leave it to the last minute to decide on photographs, etc. This would often result in a rushed and unsuccessful decision.

A 'hit and miss' style of advert designs is to be avoided!

Flexibility is also needed to allow for any changing circumstances.

- **Check Proofs**

You will need to thoroughly check and change anything which is not suitable in the proof / draft version.

You are the client and have every right to make necessary changes. You will be respected for this accuracy.

It also adds to the school's reputation.

- **Sign-off on Advertisements**

    * Each advertisement you agree on will usually require two sign-offs:
        * When the advertisement booking is made
        * Agreeing to the final draft of the advertisement.
    * The sign-off is done by the person in authority at in your school. The SMM would normally be this person who is appointed by the School Principal .
    * These are contractual documents. Be completely happy with the details before signing-off.
    * Signing-off may be done by email e.g. the radio station sends the final recordings for your approval and you reply by email giving permission for the radio adverts to be run, according to the recordings sent.

Specific Examples Follow...

Newspaper and Magazine Advertising

Newspaper Advertising

Often newspaper advertising is the most popular form of paid advertising used by schools.

It is a relatively easy form of advertising for the SMM once the background preparation is done.

Planning

As part of the SMP, it is a good method to have the themes for each advertisement's placement throughout the year decided at the beginning of the year. This will allow for appropriate photos to be taken and copy (text to be used) considered well in advance.

Each time an advert is published, ask the outlet to email you the final copy for signing-off and for your records. This also assists with future advertising requirements and ideas.

Effectiveness

The effectiveness of this form of advertising is debatable.

Using the smaller forms of newspapers, both for free and fee, will often get the greatest result of readers per dollar spent.

The free 'throw over the fence' or 'letterbox' local paper meets this criterion the best. Because every household normally receives one, there is a good chance that a good readership size results. However, at what depth? Is it just skimmed? As it is free with no financial contribution from the reader, is the reader less inclined to spend quality time reading?

The larger city, state and national newspaper publications are much more expensive and usually have a smaller readership of your targeted audience. Yet the readership has decided to purchase the paper and hence is highly likely to read it.

Carefully selected newspaper advertising could be quite cost effective for a number of advertisements over the year, particularly considering the limited number most schools would do.

It is best to also do your own research on the readership and styles of your targeted readers.

Prestige

The other aspect worth considering is that of prestige.

Some schools would see the prestige value more important than the actual number of readers. If a school is looking for a more middle / higher middle class demographic then it would more than likely want to be seen in a more prestigious publication i.e. a paper where there is a higher educated readership and a higher cost associated.

Solid Advertising Account Advantage

Having a solid advertising account will at times be to your advantage. **Financially you will gain a decent discount.**

Initially, an obvious point is that –

> the more you advertise the greater number of people will read your advertisement and therefore more people will be informed about your school.

It will also impose significantly on your School Marketing Budget (SMB).

> Positively though, you will more than likely gain in editorial / story space.

> As in any business, the proprietors will assist their best clients.
>
> If your school is in this category, you would hope for more stories from your school being published.

> You would also like to think that your school would be approached for a school's perspective on other particular stories.
>
> You would also like to be the school approached for a photo to run with another particular news story.

Advertising Consultants

You will be approached throughout the year by various advertising consultants / executives (sales people) from the various newspaper publishers inviting you to advertise. They may have an upcoming feature, special for main body advert, or a place for a 'stressed advert (see below)'.

If you have a plan (SMP), of which they are aware, then these approaches will be less frequent. It is best to advise your consultant at the start of the year about your advertising plans for their publication.

If you have no plan advised to them and you just place adverts across the publication without any particular plan, you will find that the consultant more likely thinks that you are a chance at any number of placements throughout the year. You will quite possibly be regularly approached.

'Stressed advert'

This is a system whereby the newspaper consultant needs to fill a space urgently either because it hasn't sold or there has been an unforeseen withdrawal.

It is often a good idea to advise your consultant that you are willing to use their 'stressed' advertising system.

Having a good friendly relationship with your advertising consultant, which is usually developed over the phone, often helps. This, along with your account size, is a key factor.

> The most important aspects they consider will be:
> your ability to produce an advertisement in a short time with little notification,
> along with your ability to pay.

> Stressed adverts are often considerably cheaper and at bargain prices!

Depending on their desperation and the size of your account with them, you may even negotiate the price.

S/he will give you up to a day usually, sometimes just a few hours, to create your own advertisement or get their graphic artists everything they need to create one for you.

The best plan for this type of advertising is to have advertisements already prepared or repeat a good advert already published by that outlet.

You may also have all the details and photos (photographs) ready to be sent.

You will also need various sized adverts as you never know the space size to be filled.

Magazine Advertising Overview

Magazine advertising is similar to newspaper advertising, yet the costs are usually higher.

However, a full page is considerably smaller than a newspaper's.

You need to find the best magazine which suits your school's philosophy and will accept advertisements in your price bracket.

Local magazines are often the best for schools - better target audience and less expensive.

Magazines are usually of a better print, paper and presentation quality as compared to newspapers.

Magazines usually lie around homes and offices longer than newspapers and hence have a longer lasting school marketing value.

Creating a magazine advertisement is similar to that of newspapers.

Creating the Newspaper and Magazine Advertisement - Instructions

Be prepared! Be creative! Do not rush!

Overall Tips

When creating a newspaper or magazine advertisement it is suggested that you:

- Use the school branding style.
- Be succinct and make sure the advert is not too busy (crowded with content and photos).
- Allow for the advert size impacting on how much should be included.
- Be brief. Brevity is best! A clean appearance is striking!
- Have a layout which attracts the eye of the reader - instantaneously.
- Use good photos. Relevant, striking and of a high quality in appearance.
- Use advice where necessary. Another valued opinion is often worthwhile!

Depending on the time of the year, you will need to use the theme decided upon according to your SMP - unless the plan needs updating due to changed circumstances.

Decide who will create the finished product – your school or the newspaper / magazine publisher's graphic artists.

The Plan - Instructions

- **Collect Resources**:
    * the photo/s needed
    * school logo
    * School catch-phrase / motto
    * branding graphics
    * branding style
    * branding colors

* school name in branded style
* text for the advert
* contact details and layout

- **Creative Decisions**:
  * Layout placement overall of each individual item according to branding style
  * Layout of advertising text e.g. sentence form or note form and placement
  * Relative font sizes and font styles and color of each section
  * Direction photos facing – photos should look into the page and not off the page i.e. people and structures, etc, face into the page (This draws the reader into the gist of the page.)
  * Background colors, according to branding
  * Use the advertisement size to decide – be succinct and non-busy

- **Create the Advertisement (according to the above)**:
  * If you are fortunate enough to have a graphic artist or someone with a good knowledge of publishing software on the school staff, this would be highly beneficial. You may sit with, or give a briefing to, this person who needs to be fully informed of the branding style and your advertising expectations, or
  * If you decide the publication's graphic artist will create the advertisement, you will need to send all the details plus layout design (at least a sketch) you have decided. You may give them some freedom; however make sure they are aware of the school's branding style. Emailing is quite acceptable.

Directions and Resources to Graphic Artist

- You will need to be very clear with your directions and resources presented to the graphic artist and prepared to explain these further.

- Be well prepared and accurate in your advice and resources.

- Send everything needed to the graphic artist **in one go**!

- It is not a good idea to send something later as it is very annoying to the graphic artist and could also be misplaced or misunderstood.

- A good method is to email the text and photos along with a sketched layout to either your graphic artist or the publisher's. You may have to send the sketch on 'Paint' software or the like.

- You could also present a previous advert as the general layout required and then add / show any changes.
- Have the first proof done and then evaluate. Get other opinions, if desired.
- Have necessary changes made. Evaluate the next proof. Have minor changes made. Evaluate the final proof. This should complete the process.
- You have every right to get this correct. Accuracy of branding and spelling is critical.
- When happy with the final product, the SMM should make the final call and sign-off.

Radio Advertising

It's COOL!

> Radio Advertising is considered by a major component of the community as being 'COOL'!
>
> And effective!
>
> Especially in the <45 demographic.
>
> This could be quite effective for schools with a unique angle!

For many schools this would be a foreign form of advertising.

> *As with most marketing –*
> *being one of the first to use this form in your community could work well in your favor.*
>
> *The cutting edge approach is usually beneficial!*

Cost is Relatively Expensive – Worth Considering

This is a relatively expensive form of advertising, but one which appears to be quite successful if done correctly and on the right radio station.

Often the expense is worth the overall results.

The expense occurs due to the nature of having a series of advertisements run over a short period e.g. 2-3 weeks. I believe that this is the ideal length of time for a campaign.

Individual adverts and 'live reads' are reasonable in price.

'Live reads' are partially scripted reads with a live feel, done as a discussion if two announcers are present. These sound to the listener as if the station / announcers are endorsing the school – very effective but more expensive.

These could be pre-recorded or done live.

Positives are Potentially Numerous:

> • the awareness developed in the listening public of the place of your school within the community and special characteristics the school offers

- the interest gained in a number of people to visit and hopefully more fully engage in the school
- the interest gained to at least look at your school in more detail with the possibility of engaging more permanently at a later date
- the 'coolness' factor built up within your own community
- the 'coolness' factor developed within the general public.

> Your community gains a positive sense of the school's wellbeing and place within your city / town.

Basically, it is seen as cool to go to your school.

Campaign Enhancements

The radio campaign will often include other aspects to enhance the campaign. These could include:

- attendance by the station personnel at a special event
- live-crosses to their mobile vans in the field mentioning your special event
- being at the event and advertising through live-crosses
- for a significant further charge the station could do a whole live broadcast of one of their shows from your school.

For example, if there was an Open Day in the afternoon, the morning radio show could be broadcast live from the front of your school to promote the Open Day.

This could also include fun activities for children e.g. games and prizes, plus promotional banners, large PA, etc.

> This is very effective - but also expensive.

Advertising by School, Cluster or System?

Radio advertising by an individual school is possibly best for a school in a non-capital city due to cost and relevance. (Is an advertised school in an outer suburb of a capital city relevant to a person on the other side of town?)

However, if done through a cluster of similar / denominational or localized schools, it could also be successful in a capital city. The schools may be based geographically e.g. bayside or country schools, or systemic groups e.g. Catholic or Anglican schools.

> For clusters or systems, promoting a few positives of some of the schools, often has a roll-on effect for the other schools to also be perceived positively.

Being too specific e.g. for certain order / denominational schools, could be of a disadvantage due to its minimal appeal resulting from smaller cluster, unless there was a cost-effective large enough group of schools e.g. Christian Brothers or Sisters of Mercy schools.

Audience Demographic

The radio station would need to have your target audience as its main target demographic. For young families with children up to high school age a successful demographic would be women in the 25 to 45 age bracket.

Mothers usually have the major say in selecting their school (or in fact whether to attend or not).

Advertising Times

A successful program of advertisements on commercial radio station would normally run over a two to three week period. A concentrated two week period may also be successful.

The radio slots would need to be in the play brackets which suit your targeted demographic. The best times are often breakfast and drive-home times. The next session for mothers is usually the morning session.

Suitability of Stations

Be careful of radio stations which play large groups of adverts in each advert block. Your advert could possibly get lost amongst the busyness of these blocks of adverts.

Not every station would be suitable for your school e.g. some stations have an amount of inappropriate discussion or inappropriate advertisements occurring and are recognized this way within society.

If you get tied up through paid advertising with these stations, your reputation would more than likely be adversely affected.

Be Prepared

Be prepared and organized well before your marketing period e.g. if wanting radio advertising to run in May have contract and advert slot sessions signed and sealed no later than March; preferably by February or even by the end of the year before.

Good stations usually fill their slots many months in advance.

If you leave making a decision on which proposal to accept too close to your marketing period, be aware that the consultant may have difficulty booking advert times in the sessions you require.

It may also impact on pre-recording of advert and 'live' read times.

Advertising Consultants and Proposals Plan

- Initially make contact with selected radio stations and speak with their marketing / advertising people regarding a possible radio marketing plan.
- If you don't make contact, then more than likely the radio station's advertising or marketing consultants will contact the school's SMM and request an interview to discuss a possible radio marketing plan.
- Gain proposals from 2-3 stations you would be happy to have advertise your school. These may also be based on the stations which other schools use or you feel suit your target audience.
- At the interview have a basic budget figure so that a realistic plan can be offered to you.
- If you do not want to give the figure at this stage of the negotiations you may like to give a range you are prepared to consider. (Probably allowing for a little leeway for the upper figure in later negations.)
- You do not have to accept the proposals.

- This is a good time to negotiate the number of ads, placement times and cost. There is usually some leeway from the station at this time.
The consultant will usually be able to include extra slots 'free of charge' or change some slots to better times.
Sometimes the overall cost may be reduced.

- Be professional in all negotiations and realize that there is a bottom line for the station, just as there is for your school.
- Once everything is agreed the SMM will have to sign a contract on behalf of the school to accept the proposal.
- The SMM often needs to discuss any proposal and cost with the School Principal. This is a relatively large financial commitment as part of the School Marketing Budget.

Special Event Day

A radio campaign often includes the station's attendance at a special event e.g. Open Day or Fete.

The station sets up their flags and banners, etc.

They will often have one of their vans / cars / trucks in attendance. This has their logo and colors brightly displayed. (It is often considered 'cool' by many adults and children alike to be linked with a cool radio station.)

These all help to develop a party / fun atmosphere.

There will normally be live crosses to the van personality throughout the week promoting the special event. These live crosses are often more effective if there is a continuation through the special event day.

This is often seen as very 'cool' by many people in attendance - especially the school communities. Once again this helps to develop the support of one of the key stakeholders - the school communities.

> Remember that the best marketers a school can have is its own school community members!

Creating a Radio Advertisement + Instructions + Sample

Overview for Success

The script and script reader/s are two of the most important aspects when creating a radio advertisement.

You will most likely need to use the **creative department** of the radio station to write the scripts – after presenting your basic required text.

Their expertise is in 'radio talk' and how to get a message across in an inspirational way and with the minimum of words.

Most adverts are 30-45 seconds in length.

You may like the occasional 60 second advert for variety.

Costs vary according to length and often the time slot played in.

Standard adverts are recorded in the studio prior to transmission.

'Live-reads' have a major impact on the listener. Costs for these are much higher than a recorded advert.

It is best to have specific themes.

Don't just have advertisements telling the public how good the school is.

Without themes it may appear as desperation by the school to attract enrolments.

A three week campaign will normally have 2-3 themes, often one per week e.g.:

- Week 1 - Visit the school's stand at the Schools' Expo
- Week 2 - Open Day invitation
- Week 3 - Enrolments Week

This then appears as if the school is open to people seeing how good it is and what it has to offer, with the possibility of engagement for interested new parents and children.

Scripts

The advertising consultant will usually request from the SMM the points you wish covered in both the adverts and the live-reads. If not, you will need to take the initiative – they probably don't your school or what you want highlighted.

Try to be clear and succinct and not to include too much detail. The creative people will use brevity and clarity in producing their scripts.

> You may like to try doing 30-45 second advertisements yourself to see how many words suit.
> Remember to use 'radio talk' – inflections, etc.

Once these are written by the station (see below for an example) they will normally be emailed to the SMM for proofing.

Proof these and advise them of any changes, but be realistic.

> The scripts will often appear to be too brief and you will want to add more.
>
> Be aware that a 30 second read isn't really much.
> Your best action would be to adjust what is there.
>
> Realistically, if you wish to add something you will probably have to delete something else.

Reader/s Voice

The reader/s is an extremely important aspect of the advert and needs to be decided well.

A suggestion of the people you may get to record your scripts for you:

- A personality recognized by the listeners. This could be expensive unless the personality is a past student, parent or staff member, etc.
- Students within the school. School Captains are usually a good combination, providing they have the skills. Other recognizable or successful students may also suit.
- A staff member (and maybe a student). One or both with credentials, which would be recognized or appreciated by the target audience e.g. major sporting success or a special reason for coming to your school.
- Generic people the station employs. These come at a cost, usually anywhere from a couple of hundred dollars in non-capital cities, too often more than double this in capitals.

Recordings – SMM Role

A time will be arranged for whoever is decided by the SMM to record the adverts at the station. This should be an enjoyable time for all concerned.

> It is a good idea for the SMM to be in attendance to make
> sure the recording is as expected.
>
> The SMM needs to be a calming influence.

Minor script or voice inflection adjustments are possible.

If students are involved, the SMM, or well informed designate, in most, if not all cases, must attend. This is both for support and duty of care.

A calm SMM is necessary for an effective performance by the readers.

> Radio stations should send you, usually by email, the completed agreed-to recorded
> adverts for your perusal and records.
>
> Check that these are the recordings to be used.

If these are not the agreed to recordings, or include elements not requested or required, immediately contact your consultant and arrange for adjustments before the advert goes to air.

Recording Cautions

The SMM, or informed designate, should be present during all recordings. This also allows for any inappropriate comments or misunderstandings to be rectified before going to air.

This becomes more apparent for the recording of 'live reads' when announcers have banter going with each other and maybe your students.

Live Reads and Other Cautions

However, you have little control over unrecorded 'live reads' apart from agreeing to the initial key points / 'script'.

If these are treated inappropriately by the radio announcers when going to air, you will need to contact your advertising consultant immediately and have the situation resolved.

This would usually involve extra adverts, on-air apologies, etc, depending on the severity of the inappropriateness.

Rarely an unapproved advertisement gets played. If this does happen, make immediate contact with the consultant and have the advertisement 'pulled' and replaced or rectified. Negotiated benefits to the school could occur also.

These errors on the part of the station would often see them offering to place a few more ads as compensation for you and for their good name not to be tarnished. Initially leave this offer up to them to make. If it isn't made then make contact and request some form of compensation.

Recordings for School Community / Website / On-Hold

The recordings can also be emailed to all staff, students and parents, and anyone else on your email lists.

> Most people enjoy downloading these and sharing with family and friends – an indirect form of marketing, but usually a successful one.

> Placement on the school's website is also a major advantage.

These are also good for your marketing records.

These should also be played to selected audiences e.g. Parents and Friends / Citizens Associations, School Board and Parish Pastoral Councils, etc.

> The School telephone's 'On-Hold' recording could often be a successful radio advert recording – as long as it doesn't refer to a particular event which has passed.

Copyright

Copyright – You need to obtain the radio station's permission first, if you do not own the copyright, to avoid any possible copyright infringements.

Most stations should agree that the recordings belong to the school, once aired.

Campaign Advertisement Play Time

The radio station should send the times for each day's advertising slots prior to each day. This usually happens the day before.

If this doesn't happen it will need to be followed up. These lists help you check that you are getting what you ordered. As you will not be available for all slots, try and have others also listen and report back to you.

You are also able to advise your community of the times for them to listen.

The live reads should be good presentations and effective to your campaign.

SAMPLE Follows.........

Various details have been removed to protect student identities.

LIVE READ SCRIPT:

102.9 fm
hot t●mato

Client:	
Product:	Live Read (Pre recorded interview)
Length:	29

Start Date:		End Date:	
Key No:	AQUCOL140507LIVE	Cart:	2313

Date written:	
Acc Mgr:	AL
Writer:	KH

DAY: _____

TIME: _____

Script outline only**. *Luke and Flan to record two versions each (Luke will need an extra tag)

Luke / Flan: [Captains' Names] from [Name] College are here with me... because [Name] College has got an open day from 2 to 5 this Friday... and you guys are out pressing the flesh!

Captain 1:   That's right!

Captain 2:   Sure am.

Luke: So tell me, what's so good about [Name] ...?

Captain 1:   It's friendly, supportive. It's a great place to be yourself, an individual!

Captain 2:   It's got IT centres, fully equipped laboratories, art, drama and music centers... everything you could want.

Captain 1:   Whether you want to go to uni, or do a trade, [Name] will show you how to do it... and the teachers are right behind you all the way.

Luke / Flan: Sounds like it does pretty well for a school!

Captain 2:   Oh yeah... it's way more than a school!

Luke / Flan: The [Name] College Open Day – this Friday from 2 till 5. Go see for yourself why these guys say, [Name] is more than just a school!

(Source 102.9 Hot Tomato, Gold Coast)

Television Advertising

"It's cool!" Even more cool than radio - A commonly held view by many of the school community.

> Television advertising is an expensive form of advertising.
> It is difficult to justify the expense / success ratio!
> Television is most likely seen as the coolest main-line commercial medium.

Beware: the challenges!

- **Quality**

Television advertising is fraught with various levels of the 'cringe factor' if not produced and presented in a very professional manner.

> Quality is paramount, as all weaknesses are multiplied when shown on air.

- **Large Cities**

Capital city advertising is very expensive. Similar to radio, there remains the question as to whether there is any benefit in advertising over a large area for a specific school in one location.

System level advertising would often be of benefit for those schools within the region. There is also the flow-on effect of like schools e.g. other Catholic Schools being seen as equivalent to the advertised ones.

- **Smaller Cities and Towns**

Smaller cities and towns also have the question mark over the effectiveness of this form of advertising against the cost involved. Quality of production may also be questionable.

The local television channels usually only produce a nightly news program. All other shows are normally direct feeds from the main networks. The advertising is added from the local station and interspersed with the major companies' adverts.

> The major question here is - how many people watch the local station when they could be watching the main networked station?
>
> Hence, how successful would placing local adverts through the local station be?

Television Station Advertising List – Learn from…
The best way to decide on this is to see the local channel's list of advertisers.

This is easily obtained from the station's advertising consultants. Once you have the list, check the businesses, schools and community groups, etc, which advertise.

- **Does this list inspire you to also advertise with this channel?**

It may become apparent that no really significant local or larger business accounts exist and hence there is probably little reason for you to use this form.

If the major businesses and community groups don't use it, there is usually a good reason why. This reason is most likely that the number of viewers is limited.

A case could be made for regional or system level advertising in these smaller places.

Once again, check who are the present advertisers and decide whether this suits your SMP.

Creating a Television Advertisement

The proposal

> You will usually need to work closely with either the television creative department of the station you select, or an advertising agency, to develop a professionally produced advertisement.

Professional Quote / Presentation Proposal

A good practice is to get quotes for costs along with a proposal for what each group can offer you.

A professional group will put together a proposal which would include a DVD / website downloads, etc, of successful advertisements they have created, or advertising styles they could use.

The SMM, or other key staff member / designate, will need to devote considerable time to this venture.

The School Principal, in most cases, needs to be involved with most of these processes.

It is often best for the SMM to plan with the School Principal early on the involvement s/he would like and how best to meet these requirements.

> Just as with the school's DVD production,
> it is a wonderful marketing strategy to include the fact that the school has a
> TV advertisement,
> plus excerpts from the final advertisement's production,
> in various components of the SMP.

You can always use the rider "As seen on television…" in various marketing endeavors.

SMM and Advertisement Preparations

Working in conjunction with the selected artistic group, you will more than likely need to assist the production preparation through helping to:

- develop scripts
- select and arrange scenes and props
- select actors
- develop a shooting schedule, which allows for the unexpected e.g. rain
- oversee rehearsals

The SMM, or talented and fully informed staff member, should take an active role in the whole preparation process to help achieve the desired product.

Include Your School Personnel and Facilities

The school should be involved as much as possible in the production.

> The scenes should mostly be settings from the school for authenticity.
> This helps the school be seen in a good light within the school community
> and the viewing public.

Using outside studios can give the wrong impression. It also takes away the opportunity of claiming the advert shows only your school when using other marketing forms.

Other key people and their roles within the school may be involved at different stages.

These people could include:

- Principal, overall, as well as if being interviewed or recorded as part of a scene/s
- Drama staff for cast
- Music staff for background music
- Art and Industrial Skills staff for settings and props
- IT along with Film and Television staff for graphics and some production involvement
- Other departments for classroom scenes
- Students either as lead roles or in various scenes.

SMM's Role in Production

The SMM will most likely need to:

- Oversee most aspects of the production – be Producer or Co-Producer
- Be present at all videoing times
- View the various rushes / videoed scenes to make sure these fit the desired outcome
- Work with music people to help create appropriate background music which aligns with the finished production
- Work with graphics people to obtained desired graphics
- Work within the budget and not place expectations which may have a negative impact on the budget
- Work with post-production to assist with final editing

The SMM will usually need to tread a fine line between being of assistance to the production and of being an unhelpful intrusion.

> The SMM, or designate, needs to use the skills of the experts, yet keep everyone on task to achieve the previously decided outcome.

It is best, at times, to back off, if being a diplomat is difficult or not possible in some situations.

Gaining assistance from another source e.g. School Principal or the system level Communications and Marketing Manager can often help in these situations.

School Marketing Relationships

School Marketing Relationships

One of the most successful forms of marketing can be quite low cost depending on the ability of the school to get out there and be seen.

The power of the stakeholder must never be underestimated.

Word of mouth rules. The skill is in getting the right words spoken by the stakeholders!

Building relationships within the school and school groups is essential for a successful and welcoming school.

But don't be shy! Giving your stakeholders and other interested people the facts to back your school, and for them to want to be involved, is very important!

Open Days, Information Evenings, Awards Nights, Parents and Friends / Citizens Functions, etc, along with engaging with other schools through School Visitations, are all integral to success.

Let them go away WANTING to 'tell the world' all those great things the world needs to hear about your school!

Headings

Powerful Stakeholders
School Open Day
Feeder School and Parish Relationships
Feeder School Visitation
Taster Days
Information Evenings
Awards Night / Night of Excellence
School Expos

Powerful Stakeholders

> The most powerful marketing influence in any school is the school community itself.

To have a successful School Marketing Plan (SMP) the stakeholders need to be supportive of the school.

Insiders' Views

The power of the insiders' voices to the local community is paramount. Society will more often place a remarkable amount of credit upon those who have an insider's perspective.

The views expressed by those directly involved within the school will be their personal perceptions, sometimes correct, at other times not fully informed.

In some cases negative views could be deliberately espoused as truth, for some political or retributive cause. There is an inherent need to keep the insiders informed and accountable.

Diplomacy

The School Principal, Leadership Teams, Staff, Parish Priest and other Priests need to be fully supportive of the vision and mission of the School. They need to be diplomatic in their discussions with fellow school community members and the community at large.

Confidence in the School

School Boards, Parents and Friends / Citizens Associations, and other key interest groups, should be as fully informed as possible and able to see that the school is working efficiently and fairly for all concerned.

These groups need to see that policies exist and are implemented, particularly relating to any foreseen difficulty.

Often perceptions need to be corrected through diplomacy and an openness showing that the school is working for everyone's best interest in the best way possible for a school environment.

All Schools have areas of concern, just like any other organization, yet they need to be allowed to sort out any difficulties and challenges.

Parents require certainty that problems will be addressed professionally and in the best interests of those involved.

School's Reputation is Paramount!

Children and their families need confidence in the policies, processes, strategies and endeavors of their school.

The community at large is usually either ambivalent or wish for schools to be successful environments for their children. Often society will be reluctant to support the school if this success is not being met.

When the school's main stakeholders, its community, are pleased with the school, the SMP is well on the way to success.

> The SMP is then able to highlight all of the school's vision and mission with authority. Its credibility will be high.

Never underestimate the power of the stakeholder! A recent Nielsen Global Survey also found this to be the case. In the school's case the consumers are the Parents.

Nielsen Survey Results and Extrapolation

> "Despite the ever-expanding array of advertising platforms and sources, consumers around the world still place their highest level of trust in other consumers, according to a recent global Nielsen Internet survey.

Conducted twice-a-year among 26 486 internet users in 47 markets from Europe, Asia Pacific, the Americas and the Middle-East, Nielsen most recently surveyed consumers on their attitudes toward thirteen types of advertising – from conventional newspaper and television ads to branded websites and consumer-generated content.

The Nielsen survey found that overall, consumers trust other consumers above all else! 78% of respondents said they trusted – either completely or somewhat – the recommendation of other consumers."

(*'Word of Mouth' the most powerful selling tool: Nielsen Global Survey*, 2007, The Nielsen Company, on http://www.nielsenmedia.com.au/news.asp?newsID=348)

"The Nielsen survey found that while new platforms like the Internet are beginning to catch up with older media in terms of ad revenues, traditional advertising channels continue to retain the public's trust.

(http://au.acnielsen.com/site/Trustinadvertising.shtml)

If we see students and parents as 'consumers' of what schools offer, and that they and the general public react similarly to how they do with everyday products, we could extrapolate that people in general, be they students, parents or members of the general public, trust students and parents of a particular school above all else when critiquing or evaluating that particular school.

> That is – students and parents are the greatest, trusted promoters of their particular school.

Open Day

An Open Day is a highly visible hands-on approach to introduce
prospective school children, their families and the community
to the school.
Aim to involve all groups / institutes within the school for greatest success!

Overview

An effective School Open Day would include the whole school precinct.
This would encourage the flow through of people to all aspects of the school so that
a wholistic perception is possible. Key aspects of the school's facilities, curriculum and
extra-curriculum need to be highlighted!

Reasons for attendance

People attend for numerous reasons including:

- To view and appraise a potential school for their family and child/ren
- To confirm or possibly change views they previously held
- To reconfirm the reasons they previously enrolled their child/ren at the school
- To support the school in its public presentation
- To be active participants on the day with display stands, hospitality, etc
- To support their child/ren who have a particular part to play on the day e.g. band, choir or dramatic presentations, uniform parade, stall assistance, etc
- To see what the 'school up the road' has to offer the neighborhood.

The Open Day is also open to members of the public. A well presented Open Day will
cause varying degrees of public discussion over time.

Strategies

The marketing strategy for an Open Day may include:

- Flyers delivered to houses within the school's catchment areas

- Posters – in large sizes for display in shopping centers, feeder schools and parish offices and around the school. (The school and school community need to feel a part of any major event and promote it in their own way e.g. talking at home or to friends.)
- Producing a glossy school magazine of 12-16 pages for distribution through the feeder schools for the secondary school, schools, group centers and parishes, etc
- Advertising in a selection of the local newspapers and magazines
- Advertising on a local radio station (The advertising would include key activities and times. A visit by radio station personnel on the day is a well received bonus but costs more. See Creating a Radio Advertisement in Media chapter.)
- Media releases and phone calls to key media people to try and get media to the event (See Media Releases in Media chapter.)
- Sample bags on the day, which include various School Prospectus and inclusions, paraphernalia, school DVD, etc
- Balloons handed out on the day, as well as being a part of the curriculum and display sections – have displayed on each balloon the school logo, in school colors e.g. 50/50 red and blue, and opposite colored ribbons
- Meeting and greeting by student leaders
- Tours of the school, lead by student leaders. School student leaders need to be in immaculately presented uniforms with identity badges.
- Curriculum stands for all subject areas
- Stands within each precinct to highlight particular aspects of the School e.g.
    - Pastoral care
    - Prayer and sacramental / liturgical life
    - Groups and committees
    - Pre-School facilities and activities
    - Displays from different curriculum departments e.g. IT, Math, Industrial Skills, Hospitality
    - Opening of rooms, classrooms and classes to visitors
- Performances by school musical groups / choirs, drama and music students etc
- Sporting activities
- Competitions e.g. chess, debates and sports' games
- Continual running of looped school DVD and other PowerPoints throughout the whole school precinct
- Addresses by School Principal and Parish Priest, other school representatives and School Captains – these maybe at one presentation venue or separately if each aspect of the school would like to operate individually
- Uniform Fashion Parades done in a contemporary and appealing style.

For the staged event it is important that all the marketing is targeted to the staged event's theme e.g. Open Day.

Advice on how to create and present most of the above is dealt with individually throughout this publication.

Promotional Materials:

Flyers

The flyers would encourage people to attend through an outline of the program and enticing photos. The flyer's second side should be used to highlight other aspects of the school as part of the overall SMP.

Best time

The selected time would need to be appropriate so as to attract the largest number of targeted visitors.

A balance between the different aspects of the Open Day needs to be achieved.

It is often desirable for the public to have the opportunity to see students in action, yet this would be one of many foci. If this was the aim, a good time could be a Friday from 2pm to 5:30pm.

This allows for an hour of open classrooms where best teaching practice and resources should be on view.

Displays, performances and addresses could go from 3pm until 5:30pm

If there are difficulties with students, or open classrooms aren't considered a worthwhile marketing tool, then after school or weekend open days would be more appropriate.

Venues

How much of the school plant should be opened up to the public? Each school would have their own ideas on this; however there are some guidelines which may assist:

- Open areas which would be of interest to potential students and parents
- Open areas which highlight particular stand-out physical aspects
- Use your specialists to demonstrate those particular areas e.g.
    * School and Student Offices, Meeting Rooms, Prayer / Meditation Room
    * Science and Computer laboratories, Wireless Computers, Industrial Skills, Hospitality and Restaurant, Sport, The Arts
    * Boarding Rooms, Therapy Rooms, Heated Pool, Entertainment Rooms, Dining Facilities, Car Parking

- Have an easily accessible, central, well lit area for display boards and display tables, which will allow for electrical connections for laptops and data projectors
- Use as many of the standout facilities for classes or demonstrations.

Uniformity

Uniformity of displays in line with the school's branding style is needed throughout that particular area.

The display stands, where possible, also need the same display board and table types for uniformity.

A number of parents, students and staff should be rostered to assist on each stand. Visitors enjoy talking to staff, students and the parents (within reason and where necessary under supervision).

Students should be immaculately dressed in school or performance uniform / costume.

Staff should be dressed in appropriate dress; often this would be semiformal depending on weather conditions and the image of the school.

Addresses

Addresses need to be well prepared, succinct and supported by the best quality A/V possible. Using the school's facilities will highlight the technical equipment and its use to the visitors. (Similar preparation and arrangements are need as for Information Evenings.)

Parental Involvement

It is important to have supportive parental involvement. This may be through their expertise at various stands, acting as ushers, etc, or as is often the case, through providing afternoon tea throughout the afternoon, along with wine and cheese towards the end.

Parish Open Day

You may like to consider combining all the parish resources to have a combined Parish Open Day, which would include the schools within the parish, along with all other relevant parish groups and facilities.

(See Church Marketing Manual for the Digital Age (2nd ed) 2010 for details.)

Feeder School and Parish Relationships

> Good relationships existing between the school, its feeder school/s and the parish is in itself an outstanding marketing strategy.

Improved School - Parish Relationships

When the school community and parish speak positively about, and engage with, the school, this enhances the school considerably.

For best results for the school it would generally be the **school personnel who need to be the driving force** in building this relationship.

School Leadership

This initially needs the full support of the School Principals and Priests.

These leaders need to develop the support amongst their leadership teams and staff.

The school leadership team and staff would need to actively encourage student participation within the school.

School Engagement

Some suggestions for the school:

- **Priests**
  - Priests need to be engaged and seen within the schools as much as possible e.g.
    - at school assemblies
    - staff morning teas
    - meeting students around the school grounds with teachers

- ° (Don't fear this! Students generally enjoy this and gain considerably from it. With a teacher's assistance it would be a pleasant experience once the students accept that your interest and presence is legitimate.)
- ° school / year level / class masses or other liturgies
- ° as guest speakers within Religious Education classes
- ° attending pastoral care visits with the students to hospitals, street retreats for the homeless, aged care visitations and Prep classes
- ° attending Parents and Friends meetings and Board meetings
- ° presenting at School Information Nights, Open Days, and Graduation.

- **School – Parish Liturgy and Groups**

It is through these engagements that relationships can develop e.g.

- ° Student - Staff - Priest liturgy groups to plan and celebrate weekly / fortnightly / monthly youth Eucharists. This would include students being involved with as much of the Eucharist as possible, including playing and leading the singing and music
- ° School - Parish Youth Groups
- ° School - Parish Social Justice Groups
- ° School - Parish student / young people retreats and reflection days
- ° School - Parish Street Retreats, usually at night
- ° School - Parish e/i-Newsletters / Newsletters for Youth and Families.

- **Other Key Parish Personnel Engagement**
  - ° Other key parish personnel, particularly the Pastoral Associate, need engagement with the school along similar lines as the priests but according to their areas of expertise e.g.
    - Pastoral Associate being of assistance, but not in charge of, various sacramental, prayer or pas**toral activities within the school**
    - **Age Care Director supporting the visitations by students and addressing assemblies on the benefits of these visits**
    - **Parents** assisting particular classes or students as the need arises e.g.
      - retired trades-people or interested parents assisting with Hospitality or Industrial Skills classes
      - retired business or IT people assisting with these subjects
      - other subject areas
      - coaching sporting teams
      - rehearsing students for Drama, Musicals, etc.

- **Improved School – School Relationships**

When each school speaks positively about the other school, both schools' reputations are enhanced.

- **Build Stronger School – Feeder School Relationships**

Stronger relationships between the schools are formed through a variety of ways.

Some examples are:

- Staff professional gatherings e.g. curriculum development for primary years to middle years to senior years
- Staff professional gatherings for discussion regarding student levels for primary students going into secondary school, or junior school into middle school, or middle school into senior school
- Staff spiritual gatherings e.g. Beginning Year Eucharist, Prayer Afternoons (before a social event)
- Staff social involvement with each other e.g. gatherings shared across campuses
- Secondary students:
    - ° assist some primary classes or
    - ° share their creations e.g. art, writings, with selected classes / groups from their primary feeder school/s or
    - ° a Year 12 Day occurs when the Year 12 students are involved in a number of interest areas for a morning with the primary students e.g. sport, art, reading, drama, dance, etc, on a rotational basis
- Secondary students and staff assist with primary school events e.g. Fete, Liturgies
- Primary students attend Taster Days at the secondary school
- Primary students are involved with the secondary school's Open Day, Musical, etc. And, where possible, are actually directly involved in the performances and activities.
- Parental involvement e.g.
    - ° combined P&F / P&C associations and School Boards meet regularly
    - ° each school's Principal and key staff attend / address the other school's P&F and School Boards regularly
    - ° parents are invited to key events at the other school e.g. Musicals, Open Days, Fetes, Sports' Finals
    - ° parents with particular talents in required areas are invited to address students at the other school

Priests Publicly Support Schools

The priests of the school need to publicly support each school within their Parish.

Their homilies or other addresses and the support shown for each school at that school, at the other schools and at the Parish, are very important

Principal Intervention for Non-Supportive Staff and Parents

Principals will also need to be aware of any lack of support of some staff and parents towards the other school/s.

Intervention may be necessary to allay the challenges and to show support for the other school/s.

Feeder School Visitations

Introduction

Most secondary school staff appreciate visiting their primary feeder schools to speak with their students with the assistance of a professionally produced presentation.

This helps students in the primary / elementary schools decide on the secondary school for higher school education.

The Visitation needs to be professionally produced and presented.

Role of Priests

The Parish Priest, or one of the local priests, should be a visible presence at these visitations.

Minimal presence could be as a vocal supporter of the schools at the beginning or end of the presentation.

A more in-depth presentation would have a far greater impact on the students and staff present.

This could take the form of a short PowerPoint of maximum 5 minutes placing the schools in the context of the Parish and emphasizing how we are all working together as the People of God. The schools could assist or create this PowerPoint with, or for, the priests.

As this is usually a once a year presentation to a few class groups, the Priests would be strongly encouraged to place the date/s in their calendars, due to what should be considered its high importance.

Role of School Staff

The presence and support of key personnel from both the secondary and elementary / primary schools are essential.

- The Principal of the elementary / primary school introducing their guests holds considerable weight for the students and staff present, and likewise to the student's parents when informed of the day when at home soon afterwards.
- The elementary / primary class teachers hold much influence with their classes also. How they approach the presentation before and after will have a significant impact on their students. Supporting the secondary school is essential.
  (Any personal or professional challenges these teachers may have with the secondary school need to be dealt with in other forums. These unsupportive views must not be seen by their classes. In fact, outward support is necessary.)
- The Principal of the secondary school needs to be seen as the leader by the primary students and staff. Hence, the Principal's input is essential. If the Principal is unavailable then the most senior leadership team member should replace the Principal.

The more senior the school representative the more impact can be made.

- Other key secondary personnel could include: School Marketing Manager (SMM) acting as Master of Ceremonies (MC), Head of Middle School (HMS) and key student leaders from Years 8 and 12. The student leaders would best include past students of the particular elementary / primary school being visited and / or significant personalities e.g. College Captain, outstanding sports person or performing arts student, or other well known non-elected leader from that primary school.
- Five speakers is a good number depending on the type of presentation. Too few or too many speakers will often lose effectiveness.

Year Levels Visited

The last, second last and third last years of primary / elementary school are probably the best years with which to begin the presentation. However, this will depend on the state and country. (Many families seem to decide within the second or third last years which secondary school to send their child.)

Presentations would generally be given to each student in Years 4-6 or 5-7 depending on the state and country. The presentation to the higher year levels would be to support the one they received in the younger grade.
Best not to repeat the same presentation each year –

i.e. each following year's presentation, for the higher year levels who received the presentation in a younger grade, needs to have differences yet maintain the core messages of the previous year. Don't bore your audience!!!

> Variety is needed for the students,
> but also support of the key messages for each year of the presentation.

The variation could be in the form of:

- yearly updated College DVD and PowerPoints
- updated Prospectus
- different student speakers

Presentation Overview

Visitations are usually conducted in the few weeks before the secondary school's Open Day.

Visitations are best done in the morning when everyone is feeling fresh.

Presentations are usually done for individual year levels. However, combinations may occur due to the primary / elementary school's needs.

Numbers of students attending each presentation should be appropriate. Too many students in one room at a time can easily limit the effectiveness of the morning. 80-100 students should be the maximum in a good sized room. Large auditoriums often do not suit these forms of engagement.

> The whole presentation should be for about an hour or less.
> The length would depend on the variety of resources brought from the secondary school.

Too much talk from teachers / administrators without visual aid will usually gain a negative impact.

> Primary / elementary students particularly enjoy the visual presentations,
> the secondary students' addresses and the Principal's presentation (if succinct).

Room and Facilities

> The room needs to be appropriate for the numbers of students present.
> Not too big or small.
> Good ventilation and lighting.

Facilities for data projection are also required.

It is also essential to bring a computer technician or other staff member to set up if needed and be available for any break-down moments.

Use the primary school's data projection facilities, if appropriate. This is a good PR move also.

The computer technician needs to arrive earlier to evaluate the equipment and decide on the best approach.

All data projection facilities also need to be brought by the school as a back-up in case there is a failure at the primary school. (This does happen!)

It is not a good PR moment when there is equipment failure.

However, be cool, attend to the problem and adjust the agenda to suit.

If at all possible, return to the data projection when the problem is solved. The computer expertise of the secondary school needs to be seen.

Preparation Before Visitations

- **Preparation for the Visitations requires school secretaries:**

  - Obtaining the numbers of each year level from each school to be visited
  - Counting of the required number of Prospectus and 'goodies / gifts' for each year level for each school and placing these in marked boxes per year level per school. This would also require placing all inclusions in each prospectus
  - Arranging times and dates with each school for each year level and approximate arrival times of staff and students. (Computer technician arrives about 30 - 45 minutes before the others.)
  - Coordinating these times and dates with staff attending + advising staff of meeting times and places on the day
  - Letters for parents of each student attending from the secondary school advising of the event, date and times, and transport in teachers' cars is written and left with the Principal.

- **Preparation before the day also requires:**

  - Principal, Head of Middle School and SMM usually are the people to decide on the best students to attend each school
  - Principal invites these students to attend and to prepare an address
  - Permission letters are given to the students
  - Students advised usually by the Principal of the honor of being invited, expectations when away from the College, along with uniform, hair, jewellery expectations, etc
  - The students' addresses most often are coordinated by the HMS to avoid overlapping of ideas
  - Principal may like to hear each address prior. This allows for both support for each student from the highest office in the school (hence showing the importance of such event) plus a final check of what will be said.

Preparation on the day of the Visitation/s:

- HMS checks after roll call that students are at school. If not, HMS along with the Principal, make any necessary changes
- HMS reminds students of meeting times at the Office and uniform check is done
- Secretary places boxes of Prospectus and 'goodies / gifts' out for taking
- Computer Technician finalizes equipment including:
    - data projector
    - laptop with DVD and PowerPoint presentation already installed
    - necessary leads, power boards and computer cables etc
    - large screen.
- Computer technician departs allowing for an arrival of about 30-45 minutes prior to beginning of the first presentation.
- Other staff and students leave allowing for an arrival time of about 15 minutes before the presentation.
- All staff sign-in at the primary school's office on arrival and usually go with the Primary Principal to the venue. (Computer technician may often be taken / directed by a secretary.)

Sample Visitation Presentation Agenda

A possible Visitation Presentation agenda could be:
(All speakers must remember that Brevity is paramount!)

1. MC introduces the morning (advises that questions will be invited at end of morning, depending on time available)
2. Parish Priest welcomes everyone through prayer, says a few brief words of support for the schools and where possible shows a short 5 minute max PowerPoint linking the schools to the parish/es

3. School's DVD is shown
4. PowerPoint - photos summarizing the previous year. Up to 180 photos could be shown. The MC gives an extremely short explanation of many of the photos or group of photos. 3-5 second transitions from photo to photo.
5. Head of Middle School offers a few short comments and introduces the student speakers
6. MC introduces the Principal. Principal gives a short address and distributes the College's Prospectus and talks through it. S/he invites students to the College's Open Day
7. Questions from students
8. On completion of the visit a sincere thanks to the elementary / primary Principal and teachers should be offered.

This is a wonderful opportunity for both the primary and secondary schools to further build on their partnerships.

Taster Days

Elementary / Primary students visiting their secondary school should lead to much shared joy, motivation and reputation building.

Overview

Planned days for students in the last two to three years of primary / junior school (and last year for reinforcement, if desired) from each of a secondary school's feeder schools, allows the students to experience life in a secondary school.

Having too many visiting students at any one time can be detrimental and may cause disruption to normal secondary classes.
Both primary and secondary teachers and students would more than likely feel pressurized and not fully enjoy the experience.

Priest and Pastoral Associates Involvement

Once again it is important for the Priests and / or Pastoral Associates to be seen at these unique opportunities.

There may be a place for a beginning prayer and welcome of the primary / junior students to the secondary school for the day.

Otherwise just being around at different times throughout the day and having a chat with the students as they do various class activities or around the playground during lunch is of an immeasurable advantage.

Different Experiences

Students experiencing different subjects to primary / elementary school, or different aspects of their regular subjects, should be the intention of each day.

Some of these areas could include: Graphics, Hospitality, Industrial Skills, Drama, Music / Band, Math or English through the use of IT, Advanced IT, Dance, etc.

Other physical aspects of the College could be highlighted through different activities e.g. the new gymnasium or pool, theatre, individual music rooms, workshops, data projection rooms, sacred space, etc.

Different schools visiting on different days are often easier to organize.

Day Plan

- The plan could be to have the visiting students divided into different sized groups depending on the activities offered.
- The students would then rotate through a number of the activities over the course of the day.
- Having some of the secondary students in attendance to help and be involved is an often successful approach.
- A shared lunch with the Year 7/8 students (lowest secondary level) e.g. bar-b-q and drink is appreciated by all.

Teachers

> Teachers need to be interested in, and prepared for, the event,
> for there to be a successful outcome.

Promotion of the Taster Days needs to be an integral part of the staff formation for a better appreciation of the School Marketing Plan (SMP).

Teachers taking each activity should be well prepared and be able to offer the best experience they can in their particular subject area.

> The visiting elementary / primary teachers must feel genuinely welcomed and an integral part of the Taster Day.

Transport

> The biggest expense would be the cost of buses for schools not close by.
>
> This is best paid for by the secondary school (a good PR opportunity), unless other arrangements have been made.

Information Evenings

The Information Evening better informs the parents (and students if in attendance) and hence allows for a greater appreciation and support of the school.
Information Evenings need to be well planned and executed.

Overview

These evenings are usually held near the beginning of the year in secondary schools and at various times in primary / elementary schools.

Some common secondary evenings would be: different year levels e.g. Years 12 and Year 8, and Overseas Trips e.g. Ski Trip, European Trip.

Common Primary / Elementary Evenings would be: Personal Development Programs, Grade / Class Evening and Trips away e.g. for Year 6/7.

Promotion
Parents need to be contacted a number of times to promote the evening:

- This contact is normally made through the school newsletter (e/i-newsletter) and flyer (e/i-flyer), however this is not always a reliable method
- Invitations (including e-invitations) via a school letter and / or a letter to parents detailing the advantages of the evening, who will speak and the length of time, will assist the promotion
- Emails, website promotions and even telephone calls could be used
- A reminder note is often sent home (and emailed) with their child on the day of the Information Evening.

Once a culture exists, whereby the importance of such events is supported, minimal promotion would be needed.
This would develop over time - once the relevance and necessity to parents is appreciated by them.

Time and Handouts

Time and length are critical to a good attendance. The time needs to be appropriate to your parent body with most meetings starting from 7-7:30pm.

Most meetings should go no longer than one hour. Interest and concentration is lost beyond this.

Good speakers, A/V and handouts are necessary to inform and maintain interest.

A/V and handouts should be of a:

- professional quality
- branded accordingly
- interesting and Informative

Organizers

Organizers (and assistants where necessary) will, more than likely, need to:

- collect A/V data from speakers and arrange for these to be made into PowerPoints, etc and placed onto the laptop being used on the night
- have handout publications printed
- arrange for setting up the room e.g. display table, appropriate number of chairs in a formation, wall displays, decorations, etc
- have all A/V, including the microphone checked

- arrange for everything to be set up before the end of the school day. (This allows for any adjustments or changes to be made.)

Facilities

The room should be of appropriate size, neither being too large or small, with comfortable chairs and air conditioning where available.

If the room feels empty people feel disconnected and wonder how successful the school is really is.

Place out approximate number of chairs close to the expected number of attendees - best to add more if needed, than to have too many spare.

The screen for data projections needs to be of a good size and appropriately positioned.

All A/V used must be clearly visible and able to be heard by everyone. Faint or poorly colored writing and images is not acceptable.

The lectern's height should be appropriate, as should the microphone position. Microphone needs to be able to be adjusted according to heights of different speakers on the night.

> All A/V, including the data projector and microphone, must be checked on the night before the parents arrive.

Welcoming

Parents need to feel welcomed on arrival. Having staff welcoming parents, leading them to a handouts' table and guiding them to seats is one such method.

A cheery hello and directions from staff at the door also helps.

A light supper following the presentation allows for those interested parents to stay and chat with staff and each other.

Speakers

Speakers need to be well prepared. Unless the speaker is speaking very briefly, s/he will normally have to prepare some form of resource assistance. Popular resources are PowerPoints, videos (and combinations of these) and handouts.

Having these resources made available to the organizer for inclusion on the laptop, or for printing, well in advance of the evening, is basic courtesy.

Each address should stay within the agenda and decided length of presentation.

The MC should keep tight control on presentation lengths as most audiences become agitated if the evening goes beyond the advertised closing time.

Awards Night / Night of Excellence

This is a once a year event for showcasing the outstanding generosity of Parents, staff and students to the life of the School.

A well organized and executed Night of Excellence leaves a true feel-good in those present.
As these are some of the key stakeholders, this is an exceptional form of marketing.

Venue

This is a night which needs to showcase academic excellence and effort and the visual and performing arts. Other particular aspects showing the excellence of your school could also be included.

The venue should be the best possible e.g. local Arts Centre. This adds to the occasion. Friday nights are often best as it allows for a sleep-in the next day. It is also the culmination of the week when people often feel most relaxed.

This form of venue also provides facilities and backstage personnel not usually available to schools.

Leadership Team, Invited Guests and Presenters usually sit in the front row or two. Other staff are placed from row two back.

Families need to sit together with their child/ren. When children sit together away from their parents there is more chance of noise or misbehavior. It is also quite difficult for staff to supervise large groups of children in the Front of House.

Preparation

The venue would most likely need to be booked a year or more in advance. Some schools book in five or more year lots.

Preparation begins a few months beforehand. Regular meetings are essential.

> The Principal or Deputy Principal usually chair the organizing committee – due to the significance and status of the event.

Committee members regularly include:

- Leadership Team
- Heads of IT, Art and Performing Arts
- Tickets and Trophies Manager
- Foyer Manager
- Awards Coordinator
- Lighting and Sound Coordinator
- Student Gathering Coordinators
- Staff responsible for backstage and other interested staff.

Length of Event

A Night of Excellence is best run over about 3 hours with a 20 minute intermission.

Too short in length leaves people wondering why and too long leaves the audience wanting to leave. Many will leave if it is too long.

7pm is a good starting time.

Possible Roles:

- The Principal chairs each planning meeting and drives the event.
- The Leadership Team best shares the presentation roles on the night - once again due to the significance of this most important event.
- The Deputy Principal is responsible for the efficiency of the event, organizes the rehearsal day including staffing, students in attendance, along with transport, and is MC on the night.
- The Assistant Principal (or AP / DP responsible for Curriculum) is responsible for obtaining the academic award names for each subject.
  Also responsible for obtaining nominations from staff for, and selection of, the special awards, which might include senior academic, sportsman and sportswomen, citizenship and overall top students for each year level.
  S/he writes the script for presentation of these and announces on the night the special awards e.g. scholarships to universities and technical institutes, General Excellence and Dux.
- If a religious school, the head of religion (or possibly the campus minister overseen by the head of religion) arranges and rehearses the introductory prayer often em-

phasizing the performing arts' gifts of students. This person also announces the other special awards on the night, including the senior academic awards.

- The Principal's secretary and other secretarial staff send out invitations to invited guests and trophy presenters and record replies, arrange for sponsors of each award, write the official program and arrange the printing. They arrange for programs to be on a table in the Foyer before the people arrive and distribute programs from the table.
- The Tickets and Trophies Manager arranges ticketing through the venue's ticket office; arranges for tickets to be sold through the Front Office at school and coordinates these with the venue's ticket office; distributes tickets prior to the night; arranges for engraving of trophies and collection of these and shares Foyer duties on the night to distribute any uncollected tickets.
- The Awards Coordinator and assistant check awards against award's list at school and then sequences the certificates and trophies accordingly. They arrange for transport of these to venue. At the end of the rehearsal day s/he places these in order on presentation tables which will be placed on the stage at appropriate times throughout the night. Tables would normally have clean white cloths and school logo hanging from the front of each. S/he also hands awards to presenters on stage.
- Head of IT coordinates or compiles all IT requirements onto a laptop at school and liaises with Arts Centre's Stage Manager for all IT projection requirements.
  This person, or another often being the Head of Drama / Music / Dance, would assist the Stage Manager with lighting and sound requirements at both rehearsal and on the night, and assists the Stage Manager with any lighting or sounds changes from rehearsal.
  Cool headed people are needed here. Being able to handle stressful situations and respecting the Stage Manager's right to decide are critical.
- Lighting and Sound Coordinator lists all lighting and sound requirements after collection from those staff responsible for performances on the night, and takes these to the Art Centre's Lighting and Sound Manager and explains prior to the evening.
- Head of Art selects art for the students' art display and arranges for the art, easels; display boxes, etc to be taken to the Front of House prior to opening and coordinates the set up.
- Student Gathering Coordinators arrange students in presentation order at an appropriate position usually outside of the Front of House. This is done at rehearsal and on the night. Highly efficient staff who are well respected by the students are needed here.
- Backstage staff are required to keep students in their correct places. This would entail moving them to dressing rooms, onto the stage and back to front of house. Order, calm and quietness is needed backstage.
  Often a staff member is also required to be with the Art Centre's Backstage Sound Engineer to assist those students having individual wireless microphones placed on them.
- Other staff are required to assist at rehearsals by supervising in Front of House, Foyer and outside as needed.

Rehearsals

Rehearsals are mainly held at school over the weeks prior.

The main rehearsal is often best held on the same day as the performance and at the venue.

Dividing the day into two allows for most students present only being there for half a day. This relieves stress and boredom on both staff and students in attendance. Divide the night's program in two, while staying in order.

Best to leave specialized performances and large performances with large numbers of students involved to the afternoon session.

Some schools request parents to arrange for transport to and from, and then provide school arranged transport for those who cannot be dropped off by their parents.

Permission letters to parents explaining the day, their child's involvement and time required at the venue are required well before the day.

Suggested Presentation Items:

- For religious schools - Prayer (often incorporating verbalized prayer or dramatic piece from Captains or student leaders, hymn or other appropriate piece of music played by the band, liturgical dance by best dancers to a CD and a PowerPoint presentation with backing of photos, up to 180, and accompanied by school band (or commercial reflective music – be aware of copyright), showing the year that was, with an emphasis on the religious life of the school.) Takes up to 15 minutes.
- College / School Band performing up to three pieces of varying music styles (up to 9 minutes)
- Dance item, especially any winning performance (up to 4 minutes)
- Dramatic / Monologue / Poetry / Short Story pieces, up to two, especially any winning performance (up to 10 minutes)
- Musical Performance - or a selection from the school's musical or equivalent (up to 5 minutes)
- Rock Eisteddfod (or similar type) performance – selected piece (up to 5 minutes)
- Senior Song written and performed by the Year 12 students (3 minutes)
- Changing of the Colors (Passing of the leadership roles from the present year's student leaders to the following year's student leaders - often symbolized through the passing of sashes in house colors for house captains and white for school captains; prefects are present but do not receive anything. A pledge to honor the school's principles and roles is spoken by incoming student leaders, led by the captains.)

Suggested Award Categories

The following suggested award categories would be distributed throughout the night.

Best to have a performance between each section to maintain interest of the audience and highlight each category:

- Academic Awards for Junior or Middle School
- Academic Awards for Senior School
- Special Academic and Citizenship Awards
- Sports Awards – major ones only
- Special Awards

School Expos

These days the advantage seems to be for primary schools and limited advantage for secondary schools.
Historically these were quite effective forms of marketing for both primary and secondary schools.

School Expos have a debatable rate of success for the cost.

Challenges

School parents who are considering a non-government school and who visit School Expos seem to be more interested these days in enrolling their child/ren in a school which allows them to flow into secondary school. This is easily attained through P-12 schools, but more difficult for those schools which are elementary / primary or secondary only.

The challenge to primary only schools is to emphasise the advantage of a primary education in one school and then the advantage of a progression to a secondary school.

A number of schools, particularly secondary schools, have decided to no longer participate in School Expos.

A significant challenge to secondary schools, in particular, is whether it is better to be seen at the Expo even though the amount of interest is limited.

Possible Secondary School Responses

Secondary schools may be better off having combined stands due to smaller numbers of enquiries.

Secondary schools most often emphasize the advantages of a stand-alone secondary school e.g.:
- links with feeder schools
- continuation of the Middle School philosophy into Years 7/8 and 9
- the new experience and new motivation of a new school for them where everybody starts together
- broad experience of students entering Year 7/8 from a number of schools, etc.

A number of schools, particularly secondary schools, have decided to no longer participate in School Expos.

The Stand at Expos

- **Overview**

A School Expo stand needs to be attractive, enticing to prospective parents and their children, yet not appear too busy (displaying too much).

The personnel involved in each stand are critical to its success.

  o **Leadership Team members and student leaders of schools are favoured by most parents and prospective children.**

- **SMM's Role**:
    - set up the stand during the allocated time on the day before the Expo
    - probably need to reset the stand for each subsequent day e.g. old balloons out, new ones up; tidy table and replenish display stand and table resources, including lollies
    - assist with pulling down the school's resources from the stand once the Expo is over

- **Good Inclusions**:
    - Data projector showing school DVD and PowerPoint of photos of school events onto a whiteboard screen stuck to a wall
    - Vision and Mission Statement – framed
    - Pull-up Banners (two or three) - highlighting key aspects of the school (usually a few hundred dollars in cost using key photos and school logo and motto / catch-phrase)
    - Display Stand for Prospectus and Glossy Newsletters, etc
    - Balloons - helium filled in school colours with school logo, catch-phrase, and phone and website address attached to school colored tapes and hung appropriately. Student leaders hand unattached ones out to smaller children. (Helium cylinder, commercially supplied, placed behind banners and used to fill balloons throughout the day/s.)
    - Table (for data projector and laptop, Yearbooks + some handouts. Also good for storing resources in boxes, etc underneath.)
    - School sample bags containing prospectus and inserts and various paraphernalia, and brochures and glossy newsletter placed on table and carried by staff and students to present to visitors to the stand.
    - Wrapped lollies placed in a bowl
    - Plant / flowers

Visual and Performing Arts

Most School Expos also have opportunities to exhibit various pieces of student art or for the bands, musicians, choirs, actors and dancers to perform.

If your school has talent in these areas it would be of benefit to be involved. Not only is it an opportunity for the students to perform or display their art pieces but to also showcase this particular talent to the public.

School Marketing
Resources + Instructions

School Marketing Resources + Instructions

First impressions very much count!

Two critical areas necessary as first points of contact are based around the initial contact with the school, as well as the basic resources used in all marketing campaigns.

When prospective parents, school enrolments and others in the community see or hear someone or some visual / audio associated with the School an impression is made. Make it a good one!

Often you have very little time to make an impact!

Images and people associated with the 'front' of the school are critical. From the greeting received at school, to the phone answering style and stationery used, nothing should be left to chance.

Just as important are the images, voices and sounds used in your marketing! Spend considerable time preparing for, selecting and presenting these resources.

Photos, DVDs and CDs speak a thousand words! As do the voices used in any production or conversation with the School.

Headings

Marketing Resources – What Should be Used?
Photos
Prospectus
Producing a Prospectus
Yearbook
School DVD / CD
Front Office and Staff
Telephone
TxTing
Telephone On-Hold
Newsletter
Commercially Produced Newsletter
Flyers
Posters
Brochures
Signs and Signboards
Promotional Items

Marketing Resources - What Should be Used?

Overview

Each resource could be successful depending upon:

quality and quantity of the production
expertise of the School Marketing Manager (SMM)
willingness of the SMM to explore possibilities
use of associated staff
having a suitable budget available.

Considerable Range of Resource Options

The target audience will also impact on what is best to use, and how best to produce and present these resources to the target audience. Various surveys of the target audience, e.g. Leadership Team, staff, parents and students, will assist with this information.

Discussions with other nearby schools, along with the systemic personnel, will also be of a significant assistance in choosing the appropriate marketing resources.

Examples Used in this e-Book

Below is a list of the most commonly used marketing resources for schools. These are explored throughout this e-book:

- Key Stakeholders
- Website
- Website Management Software
- Media
- School Community – priests, parents, staff and students
- Prospectus + Inclusions
- DVD / CD / Videos
- e/i-Newsletters, Glossy Newsletter and School Newsletter

- e/i-Brochures / Brochures
- e/i-Flyers / Flyers
- Photos, Photos, Photos
- Office Staff on the Front-line
- Telephone & TXTing
- Telephone On-Hold
- Email
- Signs and Signboards
- Information Evenings
- School Yearbook
- Posters
- 'Staged' Events
- School Open Day
- Taster Days
- Awards Night / Night of Excellence
- Promotional Items
- Advertising in Newspapers and Magazines, and on Radio and Television
- Internet: Blogs, Social Networking Sites, Skype, Chat Rooms, etc
- Parish Relationships
- Feeder School Relationships and Visitations
- School Expos

Photos

Photos! Photos! Photos!
"A photo tells a thousand words"
CRITICAL FOR SUCCESS!

Introduction

Never has this saying been truer than when it comes to marketing the School.
The enjoyable moments, the Baptisms and Confirmations, the successes, the socializing, the friendships, the games, the sport and the arts, the venue / school, the events, etc are recorded for perpetuity.

The photos will be used in so many ways throughout the year.

These will also be a part of recorded history.

All the forms of marketing will use selections of these photos.

Sometimes videos or DVDs / CDs may be needed as well.

If this is done properly, there will more than likely be hundreds, if not, thousands of photos taken each year.

How to Take Good Photographs – Website Examples

These days there are many suggestions to be found on the internet about how to take good photographs. A few suggestions, from when this chapter was written, would include at Kodak, BBC and Basic-Digital-Photography.com .

Doing a search of your search engine using a phrase such as 'taking good digital photos' achieves a vast variety of options.

Photos onto School Website

A good selection of these should be placed on the school's website's Gallery soon after being taken. This allows for positive discussion from the students, staff and parents, as well as being available for the whole community.

Most people thoroughly enjoy seeing photos of themselves, their peers and friends while at an enjoyable event or achieving something special.

> The School Marketing Manager (SMM) should usually be responsible for what photos are placed on the website so that these are appropriate and show images in line with the SMP.

> It is often a good practice to have the School Manager, IT coordinator, or system's administrator, as a final back up editor just prior to them placing the photos onto the webpage.

School Photographers

Taking and selecting thousands of photos per year should not be daunting.

The reasons for this will become evident once the right photographic personnel are involved and the culture of photographing most happenings is formed.

The school would be served best by having a specific person as their main photographer, along with back-up photographers for big events or for when the main photographer is not present.

These people would hopefully be staff members so as to come from an insider's appreciation of how the school operates and to save on costs.

The photographers may include the SMM, however it is often best that the SMM be a

support photographer and be someone who is available at most times for those unexpected photos. Often photographs are needed while the SMM is arranging various other happenings simultaneously.

The main photographers need a good working knowledge of photography and the camera/s they will use.

> For those special occasions not any photo will do. The setting, lighting, people in the photo and best pose, etc are critical.

Sometimes an outside professional photographer may be needed.

However, having staff members professionally trained is a viable option. The people chosen should have experience either personally or professionally from within or outside the school environment.

> Taking the correct promotional photo is an art.
> Do not skimp on this as the impact on the marketing campaign will be adversely affected.

Digital Cameras

Digital cameras are now the norm with Digital SLR cameras being the best. However, most good 6+MB digital cameras could be used for most events.

There is so much information available on the internet these days. I would suggest using your web search engine and phrases such as 'digital cameras best buys' and digital camera reviews' to access some very good information. A good review site I find is at Choice.

The DSLR camera, as opposed to any regularly suitable digital camera, should be used for special photos from main events or for photos with a special promotional use e.g. school magazines, flyers and advertisements.

Digital cameras allow for many more photos than once were normally taken with film cameras. This often allows for a better quality of photo to be selected.

> The more photos to choose from invariably allows for at least one or more to stand out in quality and relevance.

It also allows for quick selection and usage of selected photos, as well as immediate deletion.

> Virtually all the photos taken will not be made into prints.
> This will gain considerable financial savings for the School.
> Also, the digital cameras are relatively inexpensive, including the necessary DSLR ones.

Film Cameras - a Challenge

Using film cameras can cause many difficulties, the first being the availability of the film itself. Next will be finding a photographic laboratory to develop and print these. Then there is the issue of cost and time.

Having finally obtained the prints these will need to be scanned or supplied on CD for most of the uses envisaged.

This could take considerable time, which in reality is a major waste of time and money.

Digital cameras allow you to see instantly if your photos are successful and what changes you need to make.

Prospectus

The first document most prospective parents request is the school's prospectus.

It is best to also have this prospectus on the school's website in
an easily downloadable format.

You will need to decide on the number of prospectus you need printed. A good prospectus should last three years. Some schools like to change each couple of years, though. Due to the amount of time and expense involved, three years is ideal.

The prospectus production is best done in Term 1. This allows for it to be used that year, along with a more relevant use of lasting photos.

Content

The Prospectus markets key aspects of the school e.g.:

- Vision and Mission Statement
- Religious Dimension of the (religious) school / Ethical Dimension
- Curriculum available (Academic and Vocational for secondary)
- Pastoral Care, Welfare Programs, along with Pastoral Care / House / Tutor Groups
- Discipline
- Special Offerings e.g.
    * Gifted and Talented + Remedial Programs
    * IT Hardware, Software and Curriculum Programs
    * The Performing Arts, Culture and Art
    * Sport

Branding is integral to the appearance, look and feel of this document: Branding Logo, colors and design layout are essential.

Inclusions

Various removable inclusions are an important aspect of any prospectus. (See 'Prospectus Production')

Photos

Photos are also integral to the presentation and need to be of a high quality in content and production.

> People are initially attracted to the photos and then move to the text.
> Good photos encourage the exploration of the all important text on each particular page.

Photos on each page should:

- appear natural, not with a photographic studio or specially lit appearance
- be unique to that page's theme (an unrelated photo detracts from the page)
- have content which highlights a particular aspect of the theme
- normally have happy, well presented students, best to be in Years P to 5/6 in primary / elementary and Years 8-11 in secondary if the prospectus is to last three years
- include background photos which support the theme (on some pages)
- be cropped to necessary parameters to highlight aspect.

Outside photographers should be sourced if the school's equipment, photographers or creative skills are not of this standard.

Producing a Prospectus

Printers and Graphic Artists

> Most good printing firms will have professional graphic artists on staff.
> These people will do as much as is required by the SMM on the overall publication before it is printed.

You may do everything on your own software at school and give the printers your final copy in a suitable format, e.g. pdf. This is quite acceptable and will save financially, but often doesn't allow for another professional opinion. However, an opinion could be sort after first sending it, sometimes at an extra cost.

Your printer's graphic artist is often a good source for creative ideas regarding the layout, page colors, page backgrounds, photo placement, text section lengths and text fonts etc.

> A good combined approach is to use the school's ideas along with the printer's graphic artist's ideas.

Procedures

The SMM would:

- request quotes from three printing firms and request the type of support you would receive e.g. graphic artist
- Be clear about your requirements:
    * number of color and grayscale pages
    * possible number of photos per page
    * quality and type of paper
    * quality of outside cardboard or thick paper shell
    * insert sleeve
    * any tear out sections, etc.
- do initial mock-up designs of each page on either sketch paper or computer software e.g. Publisher, including placement of photos and text, background photos and colors, in accordance with your school's branded style e.g. colors, lines, swirls

and logo appropriately positioned, **but not the same for each page as this will become monotonous**

- write the text according to the predetermined themes in the required lengths; other key people could assist here e.g. Curriculum Coordinator, PC Coordinator, Head of IT (Brevity is the key.)
- select photo scenes, props and suitable students which highlight the text
- arrange for photo taking (Take many photos, varying the scene angles and students' positions and any props' positions.)
- your yearly collection of photos may have some classics which should be included (Some fantastic photos may be a year or two old. These would include those one-off photos which couldn't be taken again. A few of these will not hurt.)
- select the best photos for the layout
- gain second opinions of the text, selected photos and layout from the Principal and other key people as decided in consultation with the Principal
- proof text (Good to have key literary people here e.g. Librarian, Head of English.)
- take or email the whole proposal to the graphic artist (This would include the mock-up page designs in either sketches or digital forms, along with the digital text in Rich Text Format and photos on a disc.)
- allow the graphic artist to design each page according to your suggestions but allow them license to offer various other suggestions
- have each page emailed to you when completed and check it for layouts.
    * Proof it another time and gain second opinions
    * Make decisions and feed these decisions back to the graphic artist

---

- Best to have decisions made before asking for adjustments to avoid time wasting.

- Sometimes you may ask for a couple of variation options to look at before making the final decision. This is normally acceptable, however it shouldn't be the norm as the quote doesn't usually allow for many changes to the printer's completed pages. Most printing firms are quite good though, especially for good clients!
- have all adjusted pages sent to you for final inspection and proofing
- put together as if a complete Prospectus, and go through it with the Principal and any other key people as if you were prospective parents
- advise printer of final changes
- proof these final changes
- the SMM signs-off on the finished product
- wait one to two weeks for printing to be complete

Prospectus Inserts

A good prospectus would often have an insert sleeve for inclusions. This sleeve could also be used for other purposes e.g. if an envelope size, it could be a tear off card, with free post registration to the school on the front and a back which encourages parents to send the 'card' back requesting further information or an interview.

Some inclusions could be:

- Application Form, which includes an agreement to abide by school policies + agreement to use the child's name and photo for school purposes e.g. Yearbook and other Marketing uses
- Enrolment Policy
- Brochures e.g. Vision and Mission Statement, Support Staff including counselor and resource teachers
- Fee policy and fee structure for that or upcoming year/s
- Uniform Policy
- Special Programs e.g. Music, Extra Curricula Program, Gifted and Talented, Remedial / Supportive
- Parents and Friends / Citizens details, including any P&F/C levies
- School DVD is a major inclusion.

If the DVD is produced at and by the school's personnel, then this not only emphasizes the major points on the DVD but
shows an important aspect of the school's IT program and
skills of both students and staff.

These inclusions should be on either standard stationery or adjusted design paper, which still maintain the general branding style. The pages need to each appeal individually i.e. if each was on school stationery a sameness would be apparent.

Changes of design for these inclusions should include:

- the logo in possible varying sizes
- graphic designs maybe partially used e.g. if there are swirls normally at both the top and bottom of each page of stationery, you may just use one of these designs on certain pages
- the use of folded A3 pages is often quite effective for variety - many Application Forms are done in this way.

Yearbook

Long-lasting, informative, interesting and a special record of the school year.

Introduction

A special production which needs detailed planning.

The common length of over 100 pages for secondary and over 60 pages for primary schools is necessary to gain a good overview of the year.

It should be a main aim to include all students from that year in the publication at least once beyond the class / group photo.

Graphic Artist

A good graphic artist will save on time, creativity and stress, considerably.

Engaging a graphic artist with experience in yearbooks is a great advantage.

This person will be paid in addition to the quotes from the printers, unless you use a printing firm with a graphic artist attached.

You may engage your normal printer's graphic artist also. This would often be better value for money.

This normal printing firm of yours would also have the added bonus of an electronic record and hence access to all your published photos and texts for the year/s.

Production Timeline

Production preparation of the Yearbook is often over most of the year.

Good planning would include realistic fixed due dates for content from:
- School Principal
- Leadership Team
- Priests
- School Manager
- Campus Minister
- Staff Curriculum and Pastoral Leaders
- Student Leaders
- Preschool / Childcare Directors
- Chair of the School Board
- Chair of the Parents and Friends / Citizens Associations
- Other Committee Leaders, etc.

The staff needs to be aware of these dates.

A few follow-up reminders closer to their required due dates are essential.

Few people will be on time without follow-ups. Even then there will be some who still can't make it.

**Allow some days in your planning for these sorts of people.
Be willing to sit with them, collect ideas and produce a page for them.**

Editor

The Yearbook Editor should best be a staff member other than the SMM, due to the time consuming nature of this production.

Interested and skilled staff and students working with the SMM could be another successful model. The SMM should usually take on a part time Editor / Publisher role here.

The Yearbook Editor will need very good organization skills, interpersonal skills, literary skills, have a creative flare and be prepared to work on a whole year project.

A well planned school computer network would have the facility to store photos as soon as these are taken.

If this is the case, the Editor would explore photos when they are placed on the network by various members of the school, evaluate the quality and position these would suit in the yearbook, and then store the photos in these particular folders on their computer.

Articles should be saved on the school's network in designated folders as soon as these can possibly be written.

> Leaving writing / collecting articles / photos, etc to the last moment can cause time and production difficulties.
>
> Recalling the full possible content of the event may also be lost due to the time since it occurred.

SMM and Editor

The requirements of this job are usually too big for the SMM. The SMM will need to oversee the production.

The SMM needs to be aware that getting in the way may backfire!

Be professional, plan early with the Yearbook Editor and lock in follow-up meetings throughout the year.

It is often good to meet at least at the beginning of each month to discuss updates and to evaluate the process.

A new Editor may need considerable assistance from the SMM and other staff.

Plan for Yearbook Editor:

- Be well prepared!!!
- View a number of previous as well as other schools' yearbooks for ideas
- Meet regularly with the SMM who acts as a sounding board and who is usually ultimately responsible for the production
- Keep in contact with the School Principal either directly or through the SMM
- Obtain quotes from a number of printers and graphic artists. Often best to use your own printing firm, if at all possible, as they usually have a good feel of your requirements, know how you work, have a number of photos and stories already, etc.
- Arrange with Graphic Artist to initially meet to discuss overall plan, timeline dates for him / her, etc. Discuss possible creative features of the production including overall theme / feel and specific page layouts e.g. class photo presentation style
- Plan regular meeting dates with the Graphic Artist throughout the year. Be aware not to overdo this though. Meeting each couple of months early on, and more often closer to publication date, is often sufficient, particularly if in contact through emails and telephone.

- Develop an overall plan in consultation with the SMM, page by page to cover all key aspects of the school year book
- Decide which pages will be color. It is good to have at least the covers plus 4 plus pages in color. The more you can afford the better.
- Have a clear, realistic timeline
- Disseminate the timeline to all people involved
- Discuss with key people what is required of them and when it is required by
- Select a unique front cover that says, "This is .... (School)." Less is best though. A busy front cover distracts.
- Have a separate folder in the Yearbook folder on your computer for each page of the Yearbook
- Add to these folders throughout the year when content and photos become available
- **Do not leave things to the last minute. Too much stress! Too much chance of failure!**

Give **reminders** nearer due dates!

- Branding needs inclusion throughout, *but not the same everywhere*, as this will overdo and become less interesting – work on variations, including water-wash, partial sections of logos and colors, similar but slightly different versions of the colors and symbols and at times no branding at all, just a plan page…

- Make arrangements to send groups of pages when all details have been collected to the Graphic Artist who then works creatively and sends back drafts for your consideration
- When pages are finalized send off to the printer for printing
- Remember that good printers will have numerous other jobs on the go when you require yours done.

Therefore give the printing firm plenty of notice of your requirements and also send completed material to them when ready and when they would like it

e.g. they may be interested in you sending the Swimming
Carnival reports and photos after the event.

- Try not leaving key events out of the publication due to time constraints e.g. graduation ceremony.
- Arrange with the printers and graphic artist to have these sent as soon as possible after the agreed event/s have occurred, if these are close to publication date.

School DVD / CD

The school DVD / CD says much about the school and is often seen as 'cool'!

Introduction

The school DVD / CD need to be professionally produced. It is preferable to be produced in-house at your school for marketing, professional and educational reasons.

Whether to use a DVD or CD depends on file size of the final production. A CD is used to about 700MB and a DVD to about 4.7GB.

To be able to promote this in-house aspect using school or school IT expertise and equipment, along with staff and students, is especially good.

Purpose

- The DVD / CD content emphasize the school's:
- staff and students' IT skills (who produced the DVD)
- school's IT resources (which were used to create the DVD)
- spiritual, welfare, pastoral, sporting, artistic and cultural offerings
- facilities
- staff and students through its content and production.

Production

Many schools now have personnel who will be able to do this. Various software courses from technical colleges, universities, school systems and commercial businesses are available for interested staff.

This whole production is a **time consuming process**.

OUTSOURCED COSTS: If this needs to be outsourced commercially, be prepared for quite a large budgetary challenge.

Even outsourcing sections e.g. videoing, will be **relatively expensive**.

Production Process

Production Plan
The DVD / CD production should best have:

- a plan developed by the Producer, usually the School Marketing Manager (SMM)
- the Producer needs to take a real hands-on approach, including Directing (or over-seeing this), the videoing and overseeing music, graphics, backgrounds and editing
- a general outline of scenes, order and videoing dates and times
- leading questions for those being interviewed (preferably students, Principal, Parish Priest or other key people and sometimes staff, and given to them well in advance of taping, and discussed with them prior to recording)
- videoing done by a person with considerable competence (this may need to be outsourced if staff aren't qualified or proficient enough for this)
- graphics, especially for opening and closing scenes, interviewee names and key points being highlighted throughout as subtexts or overlays
- graphic style should be based on the school's branding e.g. as used for stationery
- background music, preferably written and performed by students or staff (and ac-knowledged in titles at end)
- a text for any overdubbing needed to complete any deficient but necessary scenes or for greater emphasis of certain aspects
- a good production length is often between 7 and 10 minutes when complete.

Videoing Skills

The camera operator will need to know:

- the camera's functions intimately
- the use of dolly rails, for moving the camera in a line while videoing
- about lighting, especially the use of natural and artificial sources, angles etc
- sound, including boom, desk and wireless lapel microphones
- the use of blue screens, which allow varied background scenes being added.

When videoing is complete, special expertise is needed for each of the following pro-cesses.

• Video Editing Software Examples
There are numerous video editing software options available at rates beginning around $US30 and going quite high.

Some video editing software examples are:

Adobe Premiere Elements 8 is a popular simple program and usually available for <$US80. See details at http://www.adobe.com/products/premiereel/

Adobe Premier Pro CS4 is a professional level program available for over $US750. See details at http://www.adobe.com/products/premiere/

iMovie for Apple users is the basic version and is part of the iShop suite available for usually <$US80.
See details at http://store.apple.com/us/product/MB966Z/A/iLife09?fnode=MTY1NDAzOA&mco=MTM3NDc5MjU

Final Cut Studio for Apple users is the professional version priced over $US950.
See details at http://store.apple.com/us/product/MB642Z/A?fnode=MTY1NDAzOA&mco=MTA4MjgwNzk

Final Cut Express 4.0 for Apple users is a smaller version for just under $US200
See details at http://store.apple.com/us/product/MB278Z/A?fnode=MTY1NDAzOA&mco=MTA4MjgwODY

PowerDirector 8 by Cyberlink is a popular inexpensive software and usually available for <$US100.
See details at: http://www.cyberlink.com/products/powerdirector/overview

VideoStudio Pro X2 by Corel is a popular inexpensive software and usually available for <$US60.
See details at http://www.corel.com/servlet/Satellite/us/en/Product/1175714228541#tabview=tab0

Advice for Hardware and Software Purchases

As the market is continually changing, and when necessary there is the need to purchase the best cost effective equipment and software, SMMs should regularly speak to:

- schools which have recently produced good video recordings
- commercial stores
- commercial videographers
- other SMMs
- Systemic Communications and Marketing Manager
- IT staff at school
- explore various hardware / video editing software reviews on the internet.

Post Videoing Sequences

The selection of best video sequences is time consuming. At least twice the length of the video / DVD taken, is needed to effectively make these selections.

(In general, a 1 hour recording will need at least 2 hours of viewing to enable a good quality sequence selections.)

- The video / DVD / 'Memory Stick' needs to be initially viewed fully with rough notes taken by the viewer on possible sequences to be used.
- Next it is viewed again with specific sequences selected and noted.
- Often another one or more viewings of the already selected sequences is needed to make the final selection of sequences that will be used.
- Editing into the chosen format is then required. The selected scenes are imported into a relevant computer software program and arranged as required on the computer.
- Graphics, photos, sound and voiceovers, along with background music are then added.

Part of School Marketing Plan

The produced DVD / CD would then become part of the School Marketing Plan (SMP).

Finished product will be made onto DVDs or CDs for distribution. (There is a multicopier available for DVD / CD copying. This is a worthwhile purchase.)

DVDs / CDs are often:

- shown on a computer monitor positioned in the School and Parish Front Offices
- embedded on to the school website or as 'You Tube' embedding (see embedding details at 'Video Uploading' section in this e-book)
- available through the website e.g. by ordering via email, telephone (or Online Shop, if this is an aspect of the website)
- sent to prospective families on request through school or parish offices
- shown to prospective students and parents and other interested people at School Open Days, Visitations to Schools or on School Taster Days of prospective enrolments
- shown as a loop in a strategic position at Feast Days, School and Parish Open Days and Information Nights, etc.
- also used for
    * Liturgy and Prayer
    * Feast Day / Open Day presentations
    * Adult Education sessions
    * Schools' Graduations

* Schools' Awards Night / Night of Excellence
* Record of School events throughout the year

Internal Promotion

Key school community members such as parents, school staff, students and priests should be made aware of this production. As well as those associated with the school e.g. feeder schools and parishes.

All should have the opportunity of viewing it.

This is a great help in building support from these groups as they see another aspect of the school and parish in action, a cutting-edge one at that.

Many people enjoy talking about what they saw on DVD / CD.

Front Office and Staff

> The first face to face contact with the staff is usually through the School Office.

Introduction

The School Office needs to depict the school's vision and mission philosophy.

This is initially done through its physical appearance and the attitude of the staff present at the Front Desk (and other staff visible from the front counter).

Nothing beats a genuine smile and open welcome.

> As with all marketing, it is the first impression which counts considerably to the overall perception of the visitor / guest / new parent / commercial representative, etc.

The School Office should be visibly welcoming, as should the Front Desk staff.
A professional appearance of both office and staff is critical.

Branding

Wherever possible, the school's branding should be apparent, for example:

- school internal colors (not necessarily school colors or outside paint branded colors)
- a branded poster of the Vision and Mission Statement
- general office layout, wall hangings and features (well designed and not cluttered)
- office staff in uniforms.

A lack of branding uniformity sends the wrong message.

The perception it creates in the visitor varies.

It may express a lack of organization or leadership.

It may say there are financial difficulties within the School or school.

To avoid any negative perception is very important.

Front Desk Monitor – Best Use of...

A good feature would be to include a monitor attached to a computer or DVD player which plays looped DVDs produced by or for the school.

The school DVDs / CDs are often the best general productions to feature.

If no quality video recordings exist, or for variety, good quality PowerPoints or similar telling various stories of the school's life would be an advantage.

Special features based on specific themes produced throughout the year have a unique place, for example the upcoming Feast or Open Days or special sacramental day or event.

Productions shown could also include PowerPoints of selected photos, which tell a particular story, for example:

- a summary of key events and happenings for that particular school year just gone
- highlights of the college musical, dance eisteddfod, dramatic science experiment, feast day highlights, etc
- grand final sporting games liturgies
- the latest purchase of key resources, e.g. new facilities, etc.
- social justice and welfare activities / fund raising
- age care visitations

Have something dynamic (moving) in the front office for people
to observe while waiting –
this should say dynamism!

Telephone

The telephone is still a primary form of communication for the school.

There is becoming a more opportune time to use TXTing for mobile phones through computer or cell / mobile dispatches.

Most people still enjoy actually hearing someone's voice when communicating. This personalizes the conversation. It often replaces the face-to-face contact / interview.

School Office Response to Calls

The telephone greeting is extremely important. This may be the first moment of verbal contact and sets the tone for the conversation. Politeness and genuine feelings of assistance need to be espoused. The school office introduction needs to include:

- a greeting
- the school name
- who is speaking and
- offer of assistance.

For example, "Good morning ... this is Leanne from St Mary's School Coomera ...how may I help you / direct your call...?"

This person should have the skills to ascertain who would best deal with the caller. For many, if not most calls, the receptionist would be able to meet the needs of the caller.

Otherwise, this would often be by noting the reason for the call and transferring the call to the relevant person's line if s/he has a line.

The call should not normally be sent directly through to the staff member without first advising that staff member who is on the line.

If the transfer was not possible, it would require taking a note of a callback number, name and short reason for the return call. This would then be passed to the staff member usually via email or telephone note placed in the appropriate location e.g. staff pigeon hole, call tray, etc.

Staff Voicemails

Key staff should have a voicemail service. Each staff member with a voicemail should include the following in his / her recording:

- a greeting
- who is speaking
- the person's role
- school name
- offer of assistance
- request for details.

For example, "Hello, you have reached the phone of Sally Fielding, School Secretary at St Mary's School, Coomera. As I am unavailable at the moment, please leave a short message and telephone number (after the beep) and I will return your call as soon as possible…"

Challenging Calls

The School Office receptionist should have skills to deal with the irate caller:

- calmness and empathy are the best tools
- acknowledge to the caller that s/he has a genuine concern
- advise that you will do whatever is necessary and possible to solve the difficulty
- pass on to the relevant person if available.

Otherwise if the person required, or someone else who could deal with the call more effectively than the receptionist, is not available, then it is best to:

- listen
- empathise
- take notes
- advise the person needing to be contacted will return the call ASAP.

The receptionist may also need to:

- just be a sounding board
- remain calm and empathetic
- genuinely sounding to offer the best advice for the solution, if appropriate.

A 'thick skin' is also sometimes a prerequisite, as well as an appreciation that the call is not to be taken personally.

Staff Response to the Challenging Call

The staff member who receives the transferred call also needs the above skills.

The telephonist needs to advise the receiving staff member of the nature of the call.

A major fear of staff is the irate caller or the call needing to be made to an irate parent.

Fortunately, experience is a wonderful thing. Once a staff member has dealt successfully with this type of call and the whole process a few times, it becomes much simpler, if not quite rewarding to handle the issue as a 'challenge'.

Remember, listen and hear, empathise, offer solution/s
if appropriate, follow-up as needed.

It is often a good idea to treat all difficulties as challenges and not problems.
Hence, challenging oneself to find a solution.

Like any challenge it is good to practice various scenarios. Staff should spend time **role playing** these types of calls (and interviews), and being evaluated and assisted by those who have the skills. This is a learning experience and not a 'test'. Those with the skills should be willing to lead these practice sessions.

Txting

Txting and School Marketing

This is a new field for most people.

However, due to the enormous use of cell / mobile phone by so many of our parents, it is now time to consider communicating to interested parents via txting.

Interested parents would be invited to leave their mobile numbers with the school office. The secretary would txt the parents as needed.

This might be for an invitation to a meeting or information session or an adjusted time for an activity, etc.

The reasons for using txting are only limited by the normal number of reasons to communicate with our Parents.

The txt messages may be delivered directly from the mobile / cell phone for individuals or smaller groups and via the computer for large groups.

Commercial Weblinks

For more information check the options in your particular country.

Some examples may be found at: White Pages in USA, Nokia in Europe and Telstra in Australia.

Telephone On-Hold

The Telephone On-Hold message is a unique way
to market the school to a 'captive listener'.

Introduction

The On-Hold message should play whenever:

- a call is being transferred to an internal line
- when the caller is placed on hold while the receptionist is waiting for a response from a staff member i.e. checking if the staff member will take the call immediately or return the call
- when the telephonist is gaining information for the caller.

Production

The message should be one recorded by, or for, the school.

Playing the radio or general music is a lost opportunity.

Using one or more radio advertisements recorded for the
school is one such good method.

Always seek written permission from the copyright owners if the School doesn't own the copyright.

This method comes across as very professional and informative. It is usually an advertisement with general content produced in an exciting format with appealing background music. (However, specific advertisements e.g. for an Open Day, are also produced for radio and might not suit this on-hold purpose due to it being out of date.)

Free Sound Editor Software

With computer software that most schools now have, quite professional quality advertisements can be the norm. A popular free sound editor software example is Audacity – see http://audacity.sourceforge.net/download/ for downloads.

Planned Recordings

School production allows for specific content to be easily used for a specific audience at a specific time of the year.

The SMM should normally have the year segmented into themes for On Hold messages e.g.: often based on key school events.

> The On-Hold message often invites telephone callers to visit the school and an invitation to explore the school's website for more details.

Script

With On Hold messages the script needs to be as succinct as radio adverts. The difficulty is the brevity required.

Key words and phrases need to pepper the sentences used.

Looped Play of Recording

The On Hold message should be a looped message of about 30-45 seconds in length. Rarely would someone on-hold be on longer than this.

If these are on longer, then a repeat of the message will emphasize it to the caller.

Newsletter

The School Newsletter is often the school's best regular form of information giving to parents and the school community.

Regular Weekly Publication

Regular weekly publication is needed for best success.

The readership should often be expanded to the parish, other interested schools and even to other willing sources e.g. parent and school businesses for display in reception rooms, offices, etc.

Website Updates

The school's website needs to be updated weekly, with each newsletter uploaded to it.

A collection of the year's newsletters on the website is appreciated by many parents and others wanting to get an overview of the year's progress.

Professional Presentation

A professional publication is needed.

The school's branding is very important and needs to be strategically positioned throughout the pages.

Photos 'tell a thousand words' and whenever possible should be used. Always include captions including details about the photo and the names of people from left to right.

Appropriate content, quality and sizing are essential for success.

Many schools use an A3 'shell' which is professionally and commercially printed and is branded accordingly. The school's photocopiers add the weekly detail to the 'shell'.

Inserts, usually of A4 size or smaller, are added for any additional information.

Effectiveness of Content

It can be argued that most people read only the front page, which is usually written by the School Principal. The most important detail needs to be included here.

It follows that the newsletter's length be appropriate so that time and money is not wasted.

A good coverage of recent and upcoming events and activities is the primary purpose of the newsletter. Include the Parish Priest's news whenever possible.

Some form of weekly rotation of topics / staff or parents presenting articles may be needed for effectiveness.

Staff, appropriate parents and student leaders should be encouraged to participate but according to certain parameters, especially length.

Brevity

Brevity is once again paramount to these stories.

This is often difficult for many people. These people need to be educated as to the best means of getting their information read in the newsletter.

> Most importantly, staff, parents and student leaders
> need to feel valued for their input to the newsletter.

Sponsorship Dilemma

Many argue that to minimize costs, the last page, or other sections within the newsletter, should be given over to sponsorship, preferably from the businesses of parents.

Others would say that if sponsorship isn't needed then a clean uninhibited newsletter can be produced. This is so that the school isn't seen as a commercial enterprise but as a stand-alone religious institute.

Many would also argue that advertisements aren't usually read.

When advertising is included in the newsletter, schools need to be in philosophical alignment with the advertising company's principles of advertising and the particular adverts used.

If the school can negotiate their own suppliers as advertisers, this should result in better success for the school, due to the often localized nature of the adverts i.e. supporting the local community and all the goodwill this generates.

Advertisements need to be carefully selected so as to not impose on the overall production. The main purpose of the newsletter is not to advertise certain products.

The decision often comes down to the school's budget restraints.

Layout Development

Schools may have one or two staff who receive and do the newsletter's layout. This is good organizational practice.

If staff can electronically send their stories this improves the time taken and in a number of ways the effectiveness of the presentation. Electronic methods would be through the school's computer networks or as an email attachment.

This method should be considered essential for economy of time and expense reasons.

The attachments should include photos, photo captions and directions to where photos are stored on any network.

The School Principal, or designated staff member, would need to decide on specific articles for each week's publication. Some articles may need to be delayed in line with the rotation method of weekly article selection.

Proofing is essential!

Commercial Newsletter

A 12-16 page professionally produced and printed commercial newsletter could play a significant role as part of the SMP.

This should also be available on the website for viewing and as a pdf document for downloading.

Introduction

This is a significantly different form of the newsletter, which has a wider distribution field, contains a large number of photos and stories written by key people within the school, and is produced at a key, or key times, within the school year.

It would be commercially printed in whatever format, paper type, etc felt best for each school.

Frequency

Due to its specialty, one or more of these publications could be done yearly. The decision would often be based on the budget, and availability of suitable content and photos.

Maximum impact should be gained due to what should be its spectacular nature!

The newsletter would highlight various aspects of the schools' life - up to the publication date/s and promote upcoming school and school events.

There are a number of suitable times of the year for publication, such as:

- End of Term 1 and before any School Expo and Open Day (a good lead in to these events, which allows for promoting each event)
- End of Term 1 / Semester 1 to link in with the school year (a neat division of the year into quarters / halves)

- End of Term 3 (just before a number of families decide to make appointments for enrolment before year's end, as well as a term before the Yearbook is available)
- Before or after the school's feast day or special school event

Distribution

The key distribution points could be:

- own school (to highlight achievements, keep school informed and further develop support for the school from its school community)
- feeder schools (to highlight upcoming or past events and achievements, keep schools informed and further develop support from the schools for your own school community)
- neighboring schools
- local commercial and professional enterprises, especially those owned, managed, etc by parents
- parish offices and churches
- diocesan expos / fairs / events, etc

Color or Grayscale

> Color pages are by far the best in appearance and hence are more enticing to the reader.

Pages come in sets of four i.e. a 16 page A4 newsletter would have four A3 sized sheets of paper folded into A4 sized pages.

A good use of both color and grayscale would be: outside and inside sheets in color, others in grayscale i.e. pages 1, 2, 7, 8, 9, 10, 15, and 16 in color.

If you were only to use four pages of color to save on costs then the outside pages are best for this.

Layout and Content

> The success of the front page is critical. Most people will decide whether to read the newsletter based on how the front page makes them feel.

A catchy Banner Title is important e.g. AQUINAS.COMmunity

The layout needs to match the branding style.

> It is necessary to have the major story as the lead story.
>
> A good photo is also essential.

This lead story needs to appeal to the great majority of readers. Some stories and photos which invariably attract attention are to do with:

- New school Principal / Leadership Team / Priest / Specialist
- New or successful welfare or social justice involvements
- Outstanding successes of sacramental programs
- Youth and Adult retreats / activities – what happens, when, who goes, benefits, etc
- Street Retreats for helping homeless and disadvantaged on the street
- 'Angels Kitchen' for helping homeless
- Welcoming invitation to new Parents to what the School has to offer
- Adult or Children's educational programs outside of normal school hours
- Outstanding successes of parents or students at cultural, educational, sporting or welfare endeavors
- Major event such as the upcoming School Musical, Sports' Final, Graduation Ceremony
- Building programs, including refurbishments
- Large expenditures / developmental programs e.g. buildings, computers
- Cutting-edge ICT developments
- Major celebrations e.g. 50th anniversary year of school or major combined schools liturgy

> Having other key stories promoted on the **front page** is very helpful to the reader.
>
> This could occur through boxed-in key words or brief summaries of stories, or captioned photos, with page numbers directing to the stories inside.

Color is also essential and appealing. Use well and often on these colored pages.
The **back page** is similar to the front page yet with different emphasizes. Color, good stories, photos and lead-in phrases or photos are needed.

This is also often where school details are displayed at the bottom of the page, often in a boxed section, for follow-up e.g. key people's roles and contact numbers, website address, school address.

Promotional boxes also work well here e.g. upcoming Open Day basic details.

> **Photos** of a good quality are the key to a successful presentation.

Once again, if photos have been taken of every event since the start of the year, there should be enough detail for the newsletter.

Full sized **school advertisements** also work well in these publications.

This is another avenue to reproduce the flyer (see 'Flyers') for Open Day previously devised.

Photographic Collages of events are also very effective.

The brushed edges of each photo in a collage based on a theme is one effective method of combining these. When done on color pages these achieve considerable success.

Some events could be: Retreats and Reflection Days, Liturgies, other Sacraments, Street Retreats for Homeless, Angels Kitchen, Sport Days, Drama, Music, Art and Dance.

Production procedures

Production procedures are similar to those for a new Prospectus (see 'Prospectus' and 'Producing a Prospectus' in this e-book.)

Flyers

Flyers target the neighboring suburbs, schools and parishes en mass.

Flyers have been found to be a very successful marketing form to reach large numbers of people in a somewhat spectacular format.

Introduction

The best approach is to have a specific theme on the flyer, which needs to be apparent e.g. Open Day, school Feast Day, social justice programs, major school events, etc.

Beware - Having a general themed flyer to promote the school will often say to the reader that the school needs more people. Many people react against this.

Purpose

The purpose is to inform the surrounding suburbs and potential families within the school of the advantages of your school to the community.

This should develop a positive discussion over time.

The prestige should be raised or confirmed. Interest should be increased with potential new families to your school and School.

Target Group

You only need to target suburbs where you are aware that students and potential students will come from.

Cost

As a general guide at time of printing, you will need to allow around 6-7 thousand dollars to print and distribute around 60 000 flyers.

Your own production costs prior to printing are on top of this.

Layout

It is best for cost efficiency to use both side.

One side would be devoted to the main theme e.g. Open Day.

The other side espouses those points you want marketed and formatted in a clear, appealing way. Some suggestions would be:

- Academic and Vocational Pathways or
- Four key areas e.g. The Arts, Pastoral Care, Sport and IT.

More than four themes could become too busy and not appear interesting enough to explore.

Quality photos, brief texts, color and branding are key aspects of any flyer.

Paper Type

Paper type is also important e.g. glossy or recycled buffed paper both attract attention but in different ways. Photocopier paper doesn't really suit this form of marketing, unless the budget is too stretched, or you have a very good quality printer.

Some recycled paper is difficult to read properly.

Font style and size, along with colors used, need special attention on recycled paper.

(Remember your branding style and colors.)

Size of Flyer

Often the best sized flyer is a double sided A4.

A high quality production is necessary.

Flyers are best not folded for distribution to the schools, school office and parishes. This often allows for maximum impact – seeing the outstanding front page.

Flyers are folded for letterbox deliveries by the printers. These are usually folded in thirds along the long side to fit easily into the box.

Delivery Methods

1. Delivery of flyers to schools and professional and commercial enterprises is also another way of keeping contact with these key personnel - Principals, Priests and Office staff. The SMM is often in the best position to maintain or improve these relationships and hence do the deliveries.

2. A reputable letter box delivery service is engaged to deliver to the chosen suburbs. These are usually found in the Yellow Pages or similar advertising publications, on the web, or through reputation.

3. Your commercial printing business would usually know of a good firm.

4. You pay for the number of houses being delivered to in each suburb. Acreages are usually charged at a higher rate.

5. Best to get quotes and negotiate the price, which is often fluid.

You order various numbers of folded and unfolded flyers from the printer.

The printer will usually arrange for delivery of the folded flyers to the distributor or for the distributor to collect from the printer. In some cases you may need to do this.

Check arrangements with your printer and distributor. You will need to make similar arrangements with the printer for the unfolded flyers the SMM will need to distribute.

Producing a Flyer

An effective flyer is similar to a double paged advertisement.

It is not a good idea to leave one side blank when it is relatively inexpensive doing a second side. Not a good idea to let an opportunity go by.

You may like to do everything onsite or send all resources to the graphic artist at the printers for completion.

Production is similar to creating an advertisement but with more detail:

- Sketch layout outlines according to decided themes and branding
- Arrange photo placement. (Each photo has to be large enough so as to clearly see the required detail. Captions are not necessary, so the photo's message must be very clear.)
- Write the text (e.g. Open Day text would need the details of the day including times, activities, displays, etc.)
- Select photos from your created file of photos for the year
- Arrange for the taking of any other photos you need
- Make final photo selections (Each photo tells a thousand words so be generous with these selections.)

Discuss layout, texts and photos with the School Principal

- Include contact details for the school, especially addresses, school website and phone number, at bottom of main page
- Proof all text
- Send sketches, photos and texts to printers for layout arranging (unless completed at the school or through a generous parent's generosity, etc – then send digital file by email or CD)
- Proof drafts received back, usually by email from printers, with the School Principal or other key personnel. Send back to printers for updating.
- Read final draft and when all changes have been made sign-off for printing.

Reminder: Arrangements should have been made as to who will get the unfolded flyers to the SMM and the folded flyers to the letterbox distributors by the due dates.

Posters

Posters are usually large, colorful and effective forms of marketing.

Creatively designed posters are eye-catching, attention-seeking advertisements.

Posters are best sized at double A3 i.e. A2

Strategically placed posters form an integral part of the SMP.

Effective Posters

Three effective posters, which do not require much preparation, are usually:

- Vision and Mission Statement
- Open Day (flyer resized)
- Information flyer (from the back of a previously produced flyer)

The Vision and Mission Statement should be displayed:

- throughout the school e.g. on the school offices' windows or display boards, in parish centers and churches, etc.

Poster Display and Production

The Open Day and information flyers' Posters could be displayed at the front of each school, in the school office, along with the Student Administration Office windows or student notice boards as well as at shopping centers.

All posters could be displayed at key events e.g. Open Day, Information Nights, etc.

Posters are best laminated for effect and longevity.

The developmental production of these posters is the same as for the Flyers.

Brochures

Professionally produced brochures highlight specific aspects of the School.

A good form of target marketing is through the use of brochures.

Key Brochures

The School Vision and Mission Statement should be presented in a brochure which is supported by posters.

Other key Brochures could include:

- Specialist Support Staff e.g. Policies and key staff for: counseling and guidance, resource staff involved with gifted and talented, remediation and special education
- The Arts and specialized offerings e.g. curricula and extra-curricular such as: school band, musicals, individual music lessons, eisteddfods, drama performances, art exhibitions and availability of visiting experts
- Sport, both curricula and extra-curricular, competitions - internal and interschool, as well as representative opportunities
- Curriculum, including academic and vocational.

Accessibility

The Brochures would need to be easily accessible. Some of the best forms of availability are:

- As an inclusion in the school's prospectus
- In display / collection stands in the Main Office
- From the key stakeholders e.g. Principal at enrolment interviews, APA / Curriculum Coordinator at subject selection interviews and information nights, Counselor, Resource and Special Education Staff and Heads of Sport, Drama, Music and Art
- At Open Days
- Information Nights
- School Expos

Other suggestions

- A good size is A4 folded into thirds along the long side.
- Branding is important, as is the layout.
- Be careful that the appearance isn't too busy i.e. cluttered.
- Wording should be succinct and informative.
- Once again brevity is important.

Production is similar to a flyer but more detail is possible i.e. more text and more photos.

Signs and Sign Boards

> Each school needs attractive, clearly visible signs stating the school's name.
>
> - along with other school details, as needed.

School Signs

These need be displayed at key points around the school's boundary.

The main entrance to the school should have the most significantly displayed sign.

If there is only one sign, it is probably best near the main entrance to the school.

Other directional signs could then direct people to other key facilities e.g. School Office, School Arts / Drama / Music / Theatre Centre, School Sporting Facilities, Pre-School, Parish Presbytery, etc.

> The lettering should be relatively large and in keeping with the school's branding style – the school name must dominate the sign.

The school's name is sometimes accompanied by other permanent information on the same board e.g. motto, significant message or school contact details.

If this is always the case at a particular school, the school must be careful not to detract from seeing the name clearly, when first looking at the sign.

Signs are primarily for locating the school and need the school name to stand out.

> Marketing the school on the same sign is of a secondary importance but still an important purpose.

Signboards

Signboards which allow for regular changing of content, and are placed in the most convenient locations for the target group to read, are good marketing forms for:

- For parents for upcoming events
- For the public for information about the school, including enrolments.

Regular Updating of Signboards

These forms of information sharing require regular updating.

The sign can quickly become an eyesore and not looked at if:

- information remains the same for periods longer than a week or
- the sign rarely has anything written on it.

> Having the sign blank for a few days occasionally is a good change.
>
> Witty comments, or other pertinent quotes, also serve a purpose, at times.

A responsible staff member or group of students should take charge for changing the board.

Usually a member of the school leadership team is responsible for the content on display. This role could be delegated to another staff member.

Large Photographic Sign

An ever increasing phenomenon is the large photographic sign.

These can be very successful, yet relatively high priced.

The content and layout are critical:

- colors and photos need to be appealing (remember branding)
- photos need to be eye-catching and pertinent to the theme/s
- key words and points are essential (sentences get lost)
- the challenge is to include all the key information and yet not allow for busyness but for BREVITY!

Professional Advice Sort

> Due to the significant expense of this project, professional advice is critical.

Spend considerable time with the suppliers / manufacturers discussing every detail including:

- size
- cost / value
- use of this form of marketing
- what works
- what doesn't work
- possible layouts
- themes for your school
- photo themes and quality
- permission to use student images, etc.

Ask the suppliers for names of other schools you could speak with and approach these schools for further unbiased information.

Schools of the same denomination as yours are more likely to relate to your questions.

> Planning the layout, content, photos and aspects of branding to be used are similar to creating newspaper and magazine advertisements.

Promotional Items

Everyone loves a gift.

Promotional items are usually forms of gifts to prospective
students and families or guests to your school.

Feel-Good Approach and Examples

Promotional items are a successful feel-good approach.

Children, particularly in elementary / primary school, very much enjoy receiving these
items.

The common successful forms when made with good quality and value:

- biros and pencils
- coffee cups
- drinking glasses
- rulers
- erasers
- fridge magnets
- calendar fridge magnets
- calculators
- stickers
- balloons.

However, the list of possibilities is quite considerable.

The cheaper forms are often placed in 'sample bags' for distribution along with the
School Prospectus and inclusions at feeder school visitations, open days, visits to secondary schools by primary students and school expos.

The more expensive biros, calculators, cups and drinking glasses are often given to visiting dignitaries and guests. Some form of these often become part of the farewell gift to
departing staff and students.

Suppliers

The cost and quality of these promotional items varies considerably.

Quotes should be obtained from a number of suppliers. It is a good practice to obtain quotes from reliable suppliers that other schools or educational systems use.

Part of the quote will include the cost of graphics i.e. the set up costs for your logo and details which you want imprinted / etched on each item.

The details you want inscribed on the items need to attract the reader to your school and include as many details as possible. Keeping these simple is best - KIS.

Often these are: logo, school name, suburb, catch-phrase / motto, suburb, website and telephone number. The minimum and often best practice is:

- school name
- suburb
- website
- phone number.

You can easily send all details via email.

Quantities are best ordered to last over 2-3 years to obtain best value. The greater number ordered the better cost per unit ratio.

Items vary in cost but a varied selection ordered for over a year's supply will usually cost a few thousand dollars all up. Shop around.

Mid to Long Term Success

This marketing method also allows the school name to have a lasting place in the life of the child and family e.g.:

- fridge magnet on the fridge at home for the year
- biro and ruler being used at school or home
- mugs and glasses used at home or brought out on special occasions.

Caution - Use of Student Images / Details

Caution – Use of Student Images / Details

Do not include students in any promotional resources unless there is written permission from the parents.

This would include yearbooks, photos on website, newsletters, etc.

All parents should give express permission, usually as part of the enrolment form, for their children's images and / or details to be used in promotional activities of the school.

If this section isn't completed on the enrolment form the school must follow it up with the parents to gain the permission.

Be extremely careful not to include at any time any details when parents expressly advise not to use the image and / or name of their child.

If in doubt seek legal advice.

School Marketing Action Plan

Time to use the school marketing plan to begin your Action Plan.

You may need to do some research before beginning to select the various strategies with which you might like to begin.

Use the samples, suggestions and instructions included in the e-book.

Work within your budget. Good things grow from successes.

Remember - the better the planning, the better the result!

School Marketing Plan Overview Sample

Define what you have to offer:

- vision and mission, personnel, curriculum, sacramental / prayer life, pastoral and welfare support programs, religious / arts / sport education, facilities, extra-curricular activities, etc
- specific ages and groups catered for - from infants to senior secondary
- future plans – programs, staffing, facilities, etc

Define your target group:

- through surveys, observations, experience, gifts and talents available / needed
- proximity to / involvement with school educational institutes – elementary / primary, secondary and tertiary + any churches
- any expansion – programs, facilities, staffing

Budget:

- realistically support the school marketing plan
- be flexible and open to growth and change as the needs arise
- continually develop over time through needs and experiences

Personnel and Talents available - including School Marketing Manager

Develop School Marketing Aims and Objectives – from previous information

Select Marketing Strategies:

- School Marketing Relationships
- School Marketing Resources (including branding, advertising)
- Using the Media
    * Internet and other Contemporary methods
    * Both for Free (Media Releases / Editorial, etc) and for Fee (Advertising)

Evaluation

School Marketing Action Plan

Define what you have to offer:

- vision and mission, personnel, curriculum, sacramental / prayer life, pastoral and welfare support programs, religious / arts / sport education, facilities, extra-curricular activities, etc

School Marketing Action Plan

Define what you have to offer:

- specific ages and groups catered for - from infants to senior secondary

School Marketing Action Plan

Define what you have to offer:

- future plans – programs, staffing, facilities, etc

School Marketing Action Plan

Define your target group:

- **through surveys, observations, experience, gifts and talents available / needed**

School Marketing Action Plan

Define your target group:

- **proximity to / involvement with school educational institutes – elementary / primary, secondary and tertiary + any churches**

School Marketing Action Plan

Define your target group:

- any expansion – programs, facilities, staffing

School Marketing Action Plan

Budget:

- realistically support the school marketing plan
- be flexible and open to growth and change as the needs arise
- continually develop over time through needs and experiences

Bryan Foster

School Marketing Action Plan

Personnel and talents available - including School Marketing Manager

School Marketing Action Plan

Develop School Marketing Aims and Objectives – from previous information

School Marketing Action Plan

Select Marketing Strategies:

- **School Marketing Relationships**

School Marketing Action Plan

- Select Marketing Strategies:
- School Marketing Resources (including branding, advertising)

School Marketing Action Plan

Select Marketing Strategies:

- **Use the Media**
    - * **Internet and other Contemporary methods**
    - * **Both for Free (Media Releases / Editorial, etc) and for Fee (Advertising)**

School Marketing Action Plan

Evaluation

Conclusion

The journey to successfully market your school is a challenging and hopefully rewarding one for all involved. The main challenge is to be well informed, well prepared and to execute well.

Keeping informed of best practice is critical.

Know what your School Marketing Plan requires. Appreciate all its components and intricacies. Be aware of important resources and be prepared to attend professional development courses.

I believe that this e-book is one such resource developed as a result of almost two decades of marketing schools. Another good resource is the interactive website at: http://marketschools.com/. These sorts of managed interactive websites will play a key role in the future for school marketing.

I invite you to continue the engagement begun with me through the *School Marketing Manual for the Digital Age (3rd ed)* and the previous *School Marketing e-Handbook: Easy to Use Guide to Market Your School (1st and 2nd ed's)* into the world of the future through this School Marketing (SMP) website.

I began this book with the challenge to you to develop an effective, efficient and creative School Marketing Plan. I invited you to engage with what the text offers through three steps:

- Initially to explore a Sample OVERVIEW of a School Marketing Plan.
- Next to study the detail throughout this Manual to gain an intimate knowledge of the 'what, why and how' of the requirements for a successful school marketing plan.
- Finally to begin your own School Marketing **Action Plan**.

May I offer you all the best with developing your Action Plan.

Your feedback is always much appreciated.

Thought - Detailed Brevity, Creativity and Experience are important keys to the puzzle!

The future waits – seize the day! My thoughts and prayers are with you.

Glossary

Ad or Advert	advertisement
Busy	the overall layout has too much detail and will not encourage further exploration
Copy	text
Live-reads	radio adverts which sound to the listener as a discussion or statement by the on-air announcer/s and hence have more credibility; follow a basic script but allow for improvisation
Looped	a visual or audio recording that is set to automatically repeat, usually indefinitely, each time it is played completely
Pics	photos
Proof	a draft
Slots	radio specific times for radio or television advertising
Stressed adverts	form of advertising whereby little notification by newspaper outlet is given for advertisement creation and placement but at a considerably reduced cost rate
SMP	School Marketing Plan
SMB	School Marketing Budget
SMM	School Marketing Manager
RMP	Regional Marketing Plan

Bibliography

Websites used, or referred to, in this book.

All websites below were viewed in February, 2010.

http://au.acnielsen.com/site/Trustinadvertising.shtml

http://au.myspace.com/

http://audacity.sourceforge.net/download/

http://blog.whitepages.com/2009/01/29/free-text-messaging-from-your-computer/

http://bne.catholic.net.au/asp/index.asp

http://download.live.com/

http://download.live.com/messenger

http://en.wikipedia.org/wiki/List_of_social_networking_websites

http://en.wordpress.com/features/

http://en.wordpress.com/products/

http://europe.nokia.com/support/download-software

http://help.live.com/help.aspx?project=tou&mkt=en-us

http://help.yahoo.com/l/us/yahoo/edit/

http://home.myspace.com/index.cfm?fuseaction=user

http://login.live.com/login.srf?wa=wsignin1.0&rpsnv=11&ct=1263351950&rver=6.0.5285.0&wp=MBI&wreply=http:%2F%2Fmail.live.com%2Fdefault.aspx&lc=1033&id=64855&mkt=en-au

http://mail.live.com/?rru=inbox

http://mail.live.com/mail/about.aspx

http://marketschools.blogspot.com/

http://marketschools.com/

http://marketschools.com/_blog/School_Marketing_Blog

http://marketschools.com/_catalog_29976/Books

http://marketschools.com/blog-conditions-of-use

http://marketschools.com/bryan_foster

http://marketschools.com/contact-us

http://marketschools.com/e-handbook

http://marketschools.com/gallery

http://marketschools.com/hints-tips

http://marketschools.com/member-login

http://marketschools.com/news

http://marketschools.com/RSSRetrieve.aspx?ID=2480&Type=RSS20

http://marketschools.com/specials

http://marketschools.com/sponsorship

http://marketschools.com/testimonials

http://marketschools.com/videos

http://messenger.yahoo.com/

http://politicalticker.blogs.cnn.com/?fbid=C66PNrCE1OH

http://privacy.microsoft.com/en-au/default.mspx

http://schoolmarketingmanual.wordpress.com/

http://scp.org.au/

http://scp.org.au/parish_contacts.php

http://signups.myspace.com/index.cfm?fuseaction=signup

http://sites.google.com/site/schoolmarketingmanual/

http://smallbusiness.yahoo.com/

http://store.apple.com/us/product/MB278Z/A?fnode=MTY1NDAzOA&mco=MTA4Mjgw ODY

http://store.apple.com/us/product/MB642Z/A?fnode=MTY1NDAzOA&mco=MTA4Mjgw Nzk

http://store.apple.com/us/product/MB966Z/A/iLife09?fnode=MTY1NDAzOA&mco=MTM 3NDc5MjU

http://twitter.com/

http://twitter.com/about

http://twitter.com/aquinasrulz

http://twitter.com/home

http://twitter.com/privacy

http://twittgroups.com/confirm.php?oauth_token=d5G5hhEuJGJVY6cwtZjO9sMuqUtch AUfGtoLzTdltDs

http://upload.youtube.com/my_videos

http://www.adobe.com/products/premiere/

http://www.adobe.com/products/premiereel/

http://www.alwaysinteractive.com/

http://www.alwaysinteractive.com/iceberg/quicktour/

http://www.alwaysinteractive.com/iceberg/video/

http://www.aquinas.qld.edu.au/

http://www.basic-digital

http://www.bbc.co.uk/arts/apictureofbritain/how_to/

http://www.blogger.com/choose-template

http://www.blogger.com/create-blog.g?pli=1

http://www.blogger.com/start

http://www.bne.catholic.edu.au/

http://www.catholicleader.com.au/news.php/schools-news/college-reaches-out_54521

http://www.choice.com.au/Reviews-and-Tests/Technology/Cameras-and-camcorders/Digital-cameras/Digital-SLR-cameras-review-and-compare/Page/Introduction.aspx

http://www.corel.com/servlet/Satellite/us/en/Product/1175714228541#tabview=tab0

http://www.crestock.com/

http://www.cyberlink.com/products/powerdirector/overview

http://www.dailymotion.com/en

http://www.facebook.com/

http://www.facebook.com/adrian.sharp2?ref=ts

http://www.facebook.com/group.php?gid=14891935948&ref=search&sid=1418024383.3181693141..1

http://www.facebook.com/group.php?v=wall&ref=search&gid=14891935948

http://www.facebook.com/help/

http://www.facebook.com/pages/Love-is-the-Meaning-of-Life/265813695571?created

http://www.facebook.com/reqs.php

http://www.flickr.com/

http://www.google.com.au/#hl=en&source=hp&q=school+marketing&meta=&aq=f&oq=school+marketing&fp=117628ddce3be56e

http://www.google.com/sites/help/intl/en/overview.html

http://www.google.com/support/youtube/bin/answer.py?answer=132460&topic=16612&hl=en-US

http://www.istockphoto.com/index.php

http://www.joeys.org/index.cfm

http://www.joomla.org/

http://www.kodak.com/eknec/PageQuerier.jhtml?pq-path=317&pq-locale=en_AU&requestid=42257

http://www.linkedin.com/

http://www.linkedin.com/createGroup?displayCreate=&trk=anet_creategrp

http://www.linkedin.com/groupAnswers?viewQuestions=&gid=2242227&forumID=3&sik=1265691816441&goback=%2Eand_2242227_13633837_1265691816439_*2

http://www.linkedin.com/myprofile?trk=hb_tab_pro

http://www.linkedin.com/static?key=privacy_policy

http://www.linkedin.com/static?key=user_agreement

http://www.loretotoorak.vic.edu.au/home/

http://www.microsoft.com/technet/security

http://www.movabletype.org/

http://www.polldaddy.com/

http://www.riverview.nsw.edu.au/

http://www.schoolmarketingaustralia.com/

http://www.schoolmarketingaustralia.com/_blog/School_Marketing_Blog/post/School_Marketing_Plan_Refreshed_for_2010/

http://www.schoolmarketingaustralia.com/ webapp 273927/Marketing the School 'Always'

http://www.schoolmarketingaustralia.com/contact-us

http://www.schoolzine.com.au/home.html

http://www.schoolzine.com.au/schools.html

http://www.schoolzine.com.au/schools/A/aquinascollege/2010/20100129/

http://www.skype.com

http://www.skype.com/intl/en/allfeatures/videocall/

http://www.skype.com/intl/en/download/skype/windows/

http://www.skype.com/intl/en/legal

http://www.squarespace.com/

http://www.surveymonkey.com/

http://www.surveymonkey.com/Home_Pricing.aspx

http://www.surveymonkey.com/Home_Videos.aspx

http://www.telstra.com.au/mobile/services/messaging/online_text_buddy.html

http://www.tumblr.com/

http://www.typepad.com/pro/#2

http://www.vox.com/

http://www.windowslive-hotmail.com/LearnMore/

http://www.youtube.com/

http://www.youtube.com/create_account

http://www.youtube.com/watch?v=nKnLepDczsM

https://signup.live.com/signup.aspx?ru=http%3a%2f%2fmail.live.com%2f%3frru%3dinbox&wa=wsignin1.0&rpsnv=11&ct=1263351950&rver=6.0.5285.0&wp=MBI&wreply=http:%2F%

2Fmail.live.com%2Fdefault.aspx&lc=1033&id=64855&mkt=en-au&bk=1263351951&rollrs=12&lic=1

https://sites.google.com/?pli=1

https://twitter.com/oauth/authorize?oauth_token=w7vv0SUaJzN5xAseicYUCXphnvZ9xpfKJIA5ePeyrXo

https://twitter.com/signup

https://www.blogger.com/start

https://www.google.com/accounts/NewAccount?service=blogger&continue=https%3A%2F%2Fwww.blogger.com%2Floginz%3Fd%3D%252Fcreate-blog

https://www.google.com/accounts/ServiceLogin?continue=https%3A%2F%2Fsites.google.com%2Fsite%2F&followup=https%3A%2F%2Fsites.google.com%2Fsite%2F&service=jotspot&ul=1

https://www.google.com/accounts/ServiceLogin?service=mail&passive=true&rm=false&continue=https%3A%2F%2Fmail.google.com%2Fmail%2F%3Fui%3Dhtml%26zy%3Dl&bsv=zpwhtygjntrz&ss=1&scc=1&ltmpl=default&ltmplcache=2&hl=en

www.alwaysinteractive.com/iceberg/

www.alwaysinteractive.com/iceberg/video/

www.skype.com

Index

6929423R00198

Printed in Germany
by Amazon Distribution
GmbH, Leipzig